I MET JESUS IN MY
BATHTUB

I MET JESUS IN MY
BATHTUB

DANENE K. SHUMAKER

MILL CITY PRESS

Mill City Press, Inc.
2301 Lucien Way #415
Maitland, FL 32751
407.339.4217
www.millcitypress.net

Unless otherwise indicated, Scripture quotations taken from the Holy Bible, New Living Translation (NLT). Copyright ©1996, 2004, 2007 by Tyndale House Foundation. Used by permission of Tyndale House Publishers, Inc.

Printed in the United States of America

Paperback ISBN-13: 978-1-6628-0772-5
eBook ISBN-13: 978-1-6628-0773-2

INTRODUCTION

While folding clothes, I prayed something like, "God, I'm asking for some guidance. I believe there's a story here, and I'm not sure what direction to take. How do I present my story? What do I tell? What do I leave out? How honest should I be?"

I hadn't been paying attention to the radio in the background. My mind had been off somewhere else. Suddenly, my ears caught something. A guy was being interviewed about his songwriting and music, and he said, "I knew I had to be completely honest about the story I was trying to tell. Otherwise, it lacks authenticity. And people are smart, and they can see through that." It could have been a coincidence, but I don't think it was.

In his article "Partakers of His Sufferings," Oswald Chambers wrote, "If you're going to be used by God, he will take you through a multitude of experiences that are not meant for you at all; they are meant to make you useful in his hands, and to enable you to understand what transpires in other souls."

I hope I am being useful in God's hands, and while I still doubt that I can ever know what transpires in other people's souls, I hope my stories resonate with at least some and have meaning for more than just me. I've been honest about the experiences I have had. The conversations are as I remember them to be but not direct quotes. I've taken some artistic liberties, but please know that my artistic liberties have not altered the stories.

I have also gone to great lengths to not mention names. This is my story, and my cohorts may not want to be part of it. They may even have different memories than I do. Everyone has a unique window they view life through. My hope is that you glean something out of the experiences I've chosen to share.

1

sat in my half-full bathtub, water from the shower running over me. I was uncontrollably sobbing—a gut-wrenching, shoulder-shaking, snot-running, crazy-moaning kind of sob. My whole life raced through my mind like a cassette tape stuck on fast forward. I wanted the water to relax me, cleanse me, and help clear my head. Instead, it beat me and suffocated me. I couldn't escape, but I *needed* to escape.

How many times had I done this to myself? Ten times? Eleven? Twenty? Too many times to count. This had to be the last time. Hadn't I promised—sworn—to myself that I wouldn't be here again?

I didn't know many emotionally stable people who sat in a bathtub crying an ugly cry when they weren't pregnant. I wasn't pregnant.

Is my daughter in the house? Could she hear me? Straining to think, I couldn't remember. In that moment, I didn't even care. Had I ever cared about anyone other than myself? The only thing I had on my mind was to figure out where I was headed.

I tried to think back to the saga that had culminated in me being in the tub. Maybe it began in my childhood when I seemed to need more than my parents were able to give. Maybe it was during college when heavy drinking was my escape and dealing and doing drugs became a way of life. Maybe it was when my perspective shifted that one night I was in Kalamazoo. Maybe it was when I began spending time with men who couldn't have cared less about me, or maybe it was when I began to use the good ones because I couldn't have cared less about them. Maybe it was my brush with death—when it became clear that my life was spared for a purpose I couldn't yet fathom. Or maybe it was this torrid affair I was currently having with a married man that had driven me to this depth.

I suppose it was a combination of it all.

I sat in that tub, and I felt nothing. I curled up, clinging to myself and weeping uncontrollably. And yet, I *felt nothing*.

I was numb.

I'd been numb for a long time because I had clung to myself, my life, my choices, and my agenda. I used empty wells to try to fill myself, but I was only filling myself up with things that made me thirst for more.

The weight of all decisions bore down on me, yet I was emotionally empty at the same time. I looked at my wrists, then at the water. I remember thinking there was no place that could be worse than where I was right then. *Had I forgotten that much?* Just a few years before, I told myself I was going to change and that I was grateful for my second chance at life.

Perhaps I had forgotten all that.

The thought of drowning or slicing my wrists scared me enough to push those thoughts out of my mind. I cried harder. My eyelids were swollen, my skin wrinkled and pruned, my tear ducts nearing empty, and snot hung from my nose to my stomach. I was even more uncertain of what to do.

2

I lie in bed
Hoping
Do you know that I'm awake?
Or care enough
To speak with me today?

—excerpt from "The Gum Wrapper"
by Danene K. Shumaker

They were up. I could hear them. Yes, I definitely heard them. They were talking in the kitchen. I wanted them to come into my room to see if I was awake. I made a coughing sound. *That'll work*, I thought. Their conversation went uninterrupted.

Maybe if I shift around a lot and make louder noises, I thought.

Nothing.

I coughed again.

Nada.

I sighed, threw back the covers, and walked out of my room and into the kitchen.

"Good morning, sweetheart! How'd you sleep?" my mom asked as she came over to give me a hug.

I couldn't tell you why I needed my parents to come into my room to see if I was awake, but it was a game I played. They, however, knew nothing about my game. How long was I going to have to lie there making little noises before they came in to see if I was up? I needed more than they realized. I always had unspoken and unrealized expectations. I was never able to tell my parents just how much attention I needed, and they never figured it out. I know now it was my parents' mental health and addiction issues that had left me feeling inadequate and neglected. I understand this now. I heard Mary J. Blige say once, "I forgive my parents for everything and blame them for nothing." I've adopted this mantra as my own.

I'd say I grew up in middle-class America. We had a nice home, which my mother kept spotless. We had everything we needed and a lot we didn't. We ate dinner together around the table at six o'clock every weeknight. I could count on hearing my father's truck coming down the road a few minutes before six. My older brother and I took turns saying grace. Mom made sure my brother and I had milk while she and my dad started in on their Manhattans.

I remember my dad being really proud that my brother was co-captain of the football team during his senior year of high school. I swam in middle school and played tennis in high school. My mom was at every meet and every game. My dad wasn't. Like many men of his generation, he didn't come to our games. My brother and I were both on homecoming court. Friends were constantly at our house swimming or hanging out. Most people I knew had the same life I did.

Making popcorn on Sunday nights before the seven o'clock movie with my dad is one of my favorite childhood memories. I always got to sit on his lap and eat out of the same yellow bowl as him, as we watched the movie together. Sometimes he teasingly brought the paper up in front of us as if to read it, blocking my view of the movie. I occasionally threw a fit, but really, I didn't care. For a moment, I had his undivided attention.

It was then when I felt safest and most secure—like we had our own little world behind that newspaper.

I grew up believing everyone wanted the best for me, even if they didn't know how to give it. In my hometown, everyone knew everyone. My parents had lots of friends, and they all looked out for each other's kids. Even the police looked out for us.

Despite that, a bunch of us started drinking in eighth grade. I think a big reason was because that's what we saw most adults around us doing, especially when they went out to have a good time. So, we drank to have a good time, too. There wasn't a lot to do in our town and drinking quickly became one of our favorite pastimes. My mother never did figure out why my best friend got sick nearly every time she spent the night.

It was easy for me to start drinking because my parents had a well-stocked liquor cabinet and a penchant for late nights. I figured out that they would not smell alcohol on my breath after *they* had been drinking.

By the time I turned fifteen, it was easy to get alcohol without raiding their cabinet. Guys at the local convenience store were more than happy to help us out if we smiled pretty and gave them a few extra dollars. Then at sixteen, I figured out how easy it was to change the "8" in 1968 to a "3" on my driver's license with a flesh-colored pencil, making it seem as if I was of legal drinking age, and I never had to ask anyone for help again.

Drinking is how I learned to deal with life. My entire circle of friends drank. One day I looked around and realized there were a lot of kids growing up in families that looked like mine—shiny on the outside, but inside we were masking pain in ways that destroyed rather than gave life.

I realize now that I was ultimately searching for peace of mind. I believe my search for peace led me to what I now refer to as "empty wells." When I found temporary peace, I was merely filling myself up from those empty wells. Yet, it's only been in retrospect that I was able to see the error of my ways.[1]

Deep down, I think we all know where our destructive paths and empty wells will end, but at first, they seem harmless.

3

"Ahhhh! I can't be late again! Especially not today," I shouted.

It was 8:30 a.m. I would have to drive. I threw the covers back, jumped out of bed, and threw on whatever clean clothes I found. Luckily, the bathroom was empty. I slid in front of the mirror and hastily brushed my teeth, then grabbed my car keys and ran out the door.

As I jogged around the back corner of the dorm and headed toward the parking lot, I saw my car. There was dew or something on my windows because they looked foggy. I looked around at the other cars. Mine looked different. Approaching the car, I saw through the fog that the driver's door was unlocked. *That's strange.*

I thought I had double-checked. I always double-checked. Sometimes I went for days without driving my car.

When I looked closer, I noticed that the fog was on the inside. When I opened the door, the smell nearly knocked me to my knees. *What was it?* I opened the door a little farther to look inside, trying to find the source. I did, and it was awful.

I checked my watch. It was 8:45.

"Damn it! Now I am gonna be late!"

My TA didn't accept late papers. Not even five minutes late. I decided to run to my class. *Who would do this? Who would take a crap in my car and rub it all over the interior? And who takes a crap that big?* No one, that's who. Seriously! Multiple animals, people, and who knows what else had to have participated. From what I saw, there was a *lot* of crap.

Yes, I really found crap inside my car that morning. It was the spring semester of my freshman year. Someone obviously didn't like me very much and had gone to great—twisted, sickening, and immature—lengths to get his or her point across.

When I got back from class, I got the phone book out. I had no idea who to call or what to say to them when I did know who to call. I decided to call a detail shop.

When the guy answered the phone, I said, "Hi, my car was vandalized, and I need it cleaned. Can I have it towed to your place? And how much would you charge?"

"What do you mean by vandalized?" he asked.

I had hoped he wouldn't ask. "Well, someone defecated in my car. I don't want to drive it, so I was wondering if you might help me if I have it towed to your place."

"Someone vomited?"

"No." I lowered my voice. "Defecated."

He laughed a little bit. "Defecated? What's that?"

Exasperated, I said, "Someone took a shit in my car and rubbed it all over the inside!"

Silence.

"Oh, ma'am." He paused. "Is it *all* over the inside?"

"I think so. To tell you the truth, I didn't inspect it. It smells pretty bad."

More silence. Then, "Wow, I've been doing this a long time. This here's a new one!"

I could tell that I would make the headlines at his next social event. You could hear the astonishment in his voice.

"So, you wanna have it towed here and have us clean it for you?"

"If at all possible," I begged more than stated.

"We charge eighty dollars for a full detail, which I am assuming you are going to need." He hesitated. "Does it run?"

"As far as I know."

"I'll tell you what," he began, a new lift to his voice. "We tow here. But I feel pretty bad that someone did this to you, and you seem like a nice young lady. I'm gonna put on one of my Kevlar suits and a mask and bring some big sheets of plastic. I'll have one of my guys drive me over there, and we'll bring it back to the shop for ya. I'd hate to have to charge ya for a tow."

"Oh no," I said. "I can't ask you to do that. It's *really* bad."

"Well, you didn't ask. I offered," he said. "You're up there on campus?"

"Yeah, Tate Hall," I said. "That is so nice of you! Thank you so much! Are you sure? Do you know where Tate Hall is?"

"Yep, right up there by Nick's. Some drunk probably thought that was real funny last night," he said. "I'll be there soon. We'll get ya set up and taken care of."

I thanked him again and again. I was truly overwhelmed by his generosity, but I doubted his theory. Having had it roll over in my mind for several hours, I had a pretty good idea who did it.

I had enough encounters with college guys to learn to put myself in the driver's seat, so to speak. When I was finished with someone, I moved on. I wanted what I wanted. One guy came to mind who might have felt particularly pooped on.

4

The highway was black, and the only light I saw came from my own headlights. The radio blared hard rock. I looked over at my accomplice who was snoozing away. We had another hour to go, so I figured I'd drive us the rest of the way home. I just needed to stay awake. I popped an ephedrine and thought about the grocery bag in the trunk.

I recalled everything that had happened earlier that evening.

With sixty-four-ounce fountain sodas and $1,200 in our pockets, my buddy and I jumped in the car, filled it up with gas, and headed toward downtown Detroit. We had the sunroof open and the sun shone in.

The music thumped and the pot, adrenaline, and caffeine were flowing. We were gonna score!

It was dark when we arrived at our destination. It was just a normal-looking house in a normal-looking neighborhood in Detroit proper, which meant that it was no posh suburb. We parked on the street in front of the house. We knew no particulars, only our dealer's first name. A very thin, stoned woman answered the door. We walked into a dim, candle-lit living room. The air in the room was thick with smoke and smelled. Some scents I recognized and some I didn't.

There were people lying down everywhere I looked. Others sat at the kitchen table to the left. They looked up and nodded as we walked past. There were bongs, spoons, bowls, papers, ashtrays, and cigarettes everywhere. I noticed a piece of rubber tubing on the coffee table. That was when I realized, *This is serious. These people are hardcore.* But it didn't stop me.

The woman showed us to a back bedroom. We closed the door behind us. That room was dark and smoky as well. Then a bowl came my way. I pulled a lighter out of my pocket, took a hit, and passed it on. Holding my breath, I started pulling out my money. All the while, we made small talk and got stoned.

The guy we'd come to see pulled a triple-beam scale out of his closet and centered it on top of his dresser. He started pulling out gallon-size bags of weed and weighing them. I usually bought a quarter ounce from someone at school, but that night we bought a pound because we decided we wanted to make money.

I look back and think it seemed so crazy—unreal, actually. We bought marijuana in a well-known drug house, in a dangerous, get-gunned-down-on-the-street kind of big city. We were about to walk out with a large, brown grocery bag hidden under a coat. At the time, it seemed like a totally normal, completely rational, and fully understandable way to make money.

We walked out, dropped the coat and bag in the trunk, and headed north.

We took a major highway home, so I looked out for cars in the rearview mirror. I was high, smoking, and smiling. The radio was cranked up, and I loved every minute of it! The only thing I thought about was the money I would make and when we'd be able to take that trip again.

5

The sun was bright and puffy, white clouds peppered the beautiful cobalt-blue sky. It was one of those absolutely perfect spring days when everything looked bright and renewed after a long, cold Michigan winter. The trees had begun to blossom, and the green leaves were a stunning contrast to the blue sky.

I got out of class and decided to head over to another friend's place to see if he was around. I met him through some mutual friends a few years earlier at a bar. I thought he might have something to smoke. I drove the downtown streets to his house, music blaring through the open windows of my car, my head banging in time with the screaming guitar riff of "Mountain Song" by Jane's Addiction.

The town was nice. Most houses I passed were freshly painted and had well-kept lawns and gardens. The residents of Mt. Pleasant put up with us college students well.

I pulled up in front of his house and finished jamming to my song. His car was there, so I figured he was home. I skipped up the steps, knocked on the door, and went in like I usually did.

I didn't see him. "Yo! You home?" I shouted.

"I'm in here!" he replied back.

I walked through the kitchen and into the living room. I expected to see him watching TV, but he wasn't. Then I thought he was probably in his room. I still didn't see him when I walked in there. Just as I was about to turn around, I spotted him. He was down on his hands and knees in front of the window on the far side of his bedroom.

I cocked my head to get a better view. "What ya doing?" I asked.

He sniffed the carpet with a short straw.

"I did a line up here last night," he said as he pointed to the windowsill. He went back to what he was doing. Then, he sat up and wiped his lip. He sniffed again, though this time more out of habit than need. He said,

"I'm pretty sure I left some for later, but I must have knocked it off."

I was stunned, but he was dead serious.

I had been to a fraternity party a few years earlier. Some people had invited me upstairs. We walked up two flights of stairs, dodged people and beer, and joined six or seven people sitting around the largest pile of cocaine I've ever seen. I was a little freaked out. As I joined the table, a thought went through my mind: *You have an addictive personality, Danene. If you never try it, you'll never know what you're missing.*

The day I saw my friend on his hands and knees, sniffing the carpet trying to get high, I thought, *Thank you, Lord! Now I know what I've been missing! An addiction so fierce I might have actually sniffed dirty carpet for the buzz!*

For a lot of people I knew, drugs seemed like the norm for them. Whenever I was around cocaine, everyone seemed like they were having a good time "bumpin' up" their buzz by adding a little more on top of whatever else they were taking.

I didn't know where the voice in my head in the fraternity house came from, but I still remember those exact words today.

Was I in that upstairs room for a reason? Did I see my friend on his hands and knees because I was supposed to? Were my circumstances speaking to me? And if so, was I listening?

6

Apparently, I did not listen very well.

I heard laughter and loud conversation. As it grew closer I opened my eyes.

"What the . . .?" asked the man walking past me, looking down at me.

Their conversation resumed, and their giggles and murmurs about what they had just witnessed now filled the air. No one offered to help me.

It was dark when I opened my eyes. I was flat on my back, lying down in a parking lot, between two cars. All I could see was the night sky, a distant light, and the sides of the two cars. *Where am I? How long have I been here?* I couldn't think straight. My brain was foggy because I was really drunk and *way* too high.

How many people saw me? What did they think? What could have happened to me while I was passed out?

I wobbled to my feet, looked around, and found my car. I got in and drove home. That was the beginning of my junior year of college. Unfortunately, that was also not the last time I found myself in a compromising position because of alcohol and drugs.

I lived a very different life from the one my parents and those I trusted the most thought I did. The version of me they knew was of a girl who aced her classes, entered art shows, worked as a DJ at the college radio station, became an art editor and then senior editor of the campus art and literary magazine, and waited tables during the lunch rush at a local restaurant three days a week. The version of me they didn't know was the girl who didn't just smoke pot, but also drank heavily most nights, messed around with pretty hard drugs and wanted to mess around with even harder ones. I stayed out until early morning, got very little sleep, and had frequent, casual sexual encounters.

My life wasn't that way in the beginning, though. That was when sex meant something. The person I was in the act with was special to me, even if the whole situation I might be in wasn't special at all. Even so, I still thought there would be a future with each one of them. I was naïve then. Otherwise, I wouldn't have slept with them.

I didn't think that way for long.

I began to truly loathe myself. I was so out of control, so immature, and so *dirty*. I didn't think. I used nearly everything and everyone in sight and allowed them to use me as well.

When did I let that start? What was the cause? Why did I think this was a good time? I'm still not 100 percent positive why, but I know it stemmed from my feelings of inadequacy and low self-esteem and self-worth that started in my childhood.

7

aughter, hairspray, perfume, and music filled the air. I was in Kalamazoo for the weekend to party with some friends from high school. A couple of us headed to a house off campus. The others went to a different party. We made plans to meet up later that night.

The house we went to was just off the main drag and it was large. A bunch of athletes lived there. I knew a couple of them from previous parties. The party was in full swing when we arrived. There were people everywhere. Someone handed a plastic cup to each of us and asked for three dollars. We all paid and headed for the keg. I milled about, talked with all kinds of people, and sipped my beer. I eventually ended up in the hallway with one of the school's star athletes. Soon everything within my vision started to slant and became distorted. I shook my head to try and get my bearings. I thought everything would straighten out.

I looked down at my cup. Not even half of my first beer was gone. It tasted normal. It looked normal, but I didn't feel normal. I was hot and sweaty and in need of fresh air. I had to hold onto the wall to keep from falling down. It was as if I was walking uphill—like the whole house was tilted.

The guy I was talking to asked if everything was all right. I told him I needed some air. People looked at me as I walked past them. Their voices sounded distorted. It was hard to walk because my knees felt like they were going to give out.

When I made it outside, I felt sick to my stomach. The cold air helped a little. I dropped my drink and the cup splintered; beer splashed everywhere. I needed to sit down.

I saw my car, staggered over, and leaned against it for what seemed like a long while. I was confused and unable to steady myself. I thought I was going to be sick. I didn't know if anyone else was around.

I was able to unlock my car door, so I slid into the backseat. I just wanted to lie down. Somehow, I had the presence of mind to lock my doors, remembering that I wasn't in a good area. Then, I passed out.

I woke up to the sound of a guy beating on my window. "Hey! You can't stay out here! This is a bad neighborhood. Unlock the door so I can help you! Come inside, where you'll be safe!"

I waved him away and fell back into the seat.

"Danene! Unlock the door!"

I woke up again to the same guy beating on my window. It was the guy from the hallway.

"You can't stay in here. This is a bad area. You need to come inside, where it's safe! Unlock the door!"

"Leave me alone," I slurred. "I'm fine. I just need to sleep."

It was dark outside the next time I woke up. The streetlights were on. The same guy was insisting that I go inside. He kept pounding on my window and telling me to unlock my car. He told me how unsafe I was in it and how safe I would be in the house. What he said made sense. It *was* a bad neighborhood. I decided I would be safer inside.

I sat up and managed to unlock the door. He opened it, held out his hand, and helped me inside.

The next thing I remember was choking. I needed to get up. I struggled but couldn't do it. The guy who had helped me out of my car was on top of me. I was on a bed in a dark room. I was trapped. All I could see was his chest. I realized I was naked. Only then did I understand what was happening. He was raping me. I coughed and choked again. Then I vomited. He had my arms pinned down. I think I tried to fight him, but I was so weak. Then everything went black.

The next thing I remember is sunshine coming through the dirty, broken blinds. It cast slits of light across my face. I didn't know where I was. The stench was awful.

I cautiously lifted my head up from the bed. My hair was stiff from vomit and I could feel it on the side of my face. I was naked. I looked around and saw that the room was a mess. He was asleep next to me. I was surprised by how peaceful and innocent he looked. Memories from the night before started to come back.

I looked around, trying to get my bearings and not wanting to wake him. I saw my clothes strewn about the room. I slipped off the bed, grabbed them, and headed for the door. All I wanted to do was get out of there. I reached for the doorknob. "Leaving so soon?" I heard him ask.

His voice startled me. I turned around to see him smiling. It wasn't a devilish smile; in fact, he looked sincere. I looked at the bed and the vomit. *What's wrong with this guy?* He acted like everything was normal—like I was his girlfriend or something.

With my clothes in a heap in front of me, I said nothing. I just opened the door and found the bathroom. I slipped inside, locked the door, splashed my face, got dressed, and left. No one else seemed to be around and he never came out of the room.

I didn't remember driving to my parents' house. I was thankful they were away for the weekend. I sat on the floor of their shower and felt so guilty. *What exactly happened? How did I let that happen? Why didn't I go to the other party? Why didn't I stay in the car? Why did I unlock the door? Why didn't I fight him more? Why, why, why?*

I had talked to that guy before. We hung out on a couple different occasions. I thought he was my friend. I tried to make sense of it in my head. I tried to rationalize it and make it seem like it was something other than rape. I had already started to do that whole head-trip thing of putting myself back in his bedroom. *Maybe I had done something to deserve what happened to me.*

I didn't want to talk about that experience with anyone. I'd heard what they do to victims of rape on a witness stand. I was so ashamed. I felt dirty—like a piece of trash. I just sat in the shower for a long time.

I was numb, unable to move, wanting all the filth to wash away.

> And like a gum wrapper
> Cast aside, I am
> Drifting along the road, I am
> Going somewhere
> But never to where I want

> —excerpt from "The Gum Wrapper"
> by Danene K. Shumaker

I don't remember crying. It was as if I had become too disconnected for that. It was in that moment that I promised myself I would not be victimized again.

I was naïve when I started college. I had been sheltered from the world. My parents rarely left the city limits of my hometown. Aside from yearly vacations and their winter home in Florida, my parents were born and raised within a fifteen-mile radius of where I grew up. Both parents passed away in that same town. That spoke volumes of my lack of knowledge concerning the world outside my small town and how everything worked.

In college—away from that small town—things weren't the same. My parents sent me to get an education, but my experiences weren't the kind of education they had in mind. People didn't watch out for me. I learned I had to watch out for myself. Although I rarely did.

In the shower, mortar was slathered between the rocks of the wall I was building, which served as my protection. I continued to build on that wall for years. I vowed I would be in control.

It was after this experience that I began to think of sex as an act wholly separate from love. It was something that could inflict a great amount of pain if I allowed myself to feel any emotional attachment. I couldn't allow myself to feel those emotions. Feelings made me vulnerable. Vulnerability made me powerless. Every last bit of naïveté and trust was gone, and I was secure in nothing.

Who could I turn to? There was no one. I couldn't talk to my parents about anything. My mother had an uncanny ability to make everything about her. And truthfully, I thought everyone else was in the same boat as me. I mean, I didn't believe any of my friends had it together enough that they could help me. And that would take trust, and trust would have opened me up too much. I preferred to keep up a facade. I didn't think I was worth good things, and I no longer wanted to care.

So, I filled myself up with things that were only going to make me thirst for more.

8

dated a good guy for a while in college. Our relationship was fine, but I grew restless and couldn't put my finger on the reason. As it turned out, I was not interested in *good*. There was nothing for me to save in someone who is good and has their act together. So, I searched (searching while still with someone was so typical of me).

When I got back from that weekend in Kalamazoo, I buried what happened deep inside me. I wondered if my boyfriend noticed there was something different about me. I wondered if he felt as disconnected to me as I did from him.

The guy who raped me called me about eight months after the incident. I couldn't believe it when I answered the phone. I felt my chest immediately tighten. I struggled to breathe. He didn't understand why I was hostile toward him. He said he called to see if we could hang out sometime. That threw me for a loop.

He had forced himself on me! He didn't wait until it was given. He forced himself with the aid of a date rape drug. What does it say about someone who would rather take it?

My boyfriend did know there was something different about me when he got back from a weekend home a few weeks later. He found me catatonic in a closet. Well, maybe that's a stretch. I am not sure I was completely catatonic—perhaps just highly unresponsive and unbathed. My parents were alerted. I was taken to a psychiatrist and prescribed antidepressants. I think that did help me get through that whole period of my life.

The psychiatrist looked at me in session one day and said, "You do realize that you could have been naked, dancing on top of a table, and still not deserve what happened to you, don't you?" That really helped me begin to put the rape behind me.

I started to believe it wasn't my fault, but I didn't feel completely set free because I still craved emotionally unavailable men. I had a good guy waiting at home for me, willing to do anything to help me, but I wanted guys who didn't want me.

Soon after, I found myself headed to the railroad tracks with someone new. We held hands, laughed, and walked down the middle of the street with pennies in hand to set on the tracks. I had no idea we were being followed.

Several hours later, I walked back through the door of my boyfriend's apartment. He was pacing the floor, running his fingers through his hair, and looking extremely upset. "I saw you tonight!" He practically spat at me.

I sat down on his couch. *Oh, God, here we go.* I did not give a damn. I didn't want to talk about it or deal with it. I did not feel a thing while I watched his mouth move and his frantic, angry gestures. I did not hear a word he said. I didn't understand or care that he was hurt.

I had been with him for two years. We were unofficially living together. Everyone loved him. He was kind and honest, hardworking and ambitious, and smart and handsome. He was a really great guy. I broke his heart and I couldn't have cared less.

The phrase "It's not you. It's me," rang very true for that period of my life.

I moved on to the next game—the next deal. I didn't care about anyone I left behind.

Were those signs that I was a narcissist or at least had some tendencies? Or was it simply a product of my upbringing? Science says narcissists are incapable or at least unwilling to question and inquire within.

9

always assumed I would get married and do the whole family thing at some point. I just never gave it much thought. Then suddenly, my new boyfriend (the one I dumped my old one for) and I decided to get married right out of college. That was yet another example of my great decision-making skills. We were at my friend's apartment in Ann Arbor when we decided to tell people about our wedding plans. I remember one of my friends from college asked, "Really?"

The story of how I met this boyfriend was interesting. I was going to supply a huge party with LSD. So, my order was especially large, which made me kind of nervous. When I went to see my dealer, a guy with dark, round sunglasses was in the corner. That was the first time I saw him. I thought the guy might be a narc since I'd never saw him before. He sat in the corner without saying a word, with his arms and legs crossed. And he had a tie on.

I used my head to direct my dealer toward him. "Is he all right?" I asked in a whisper.

She replied, "Relax. He's cool."

I think I was trying to break out of what was "typical" for me when I met him. He may have been a stoner, but he was clean cut and dressed well. I wondered if any of the guys I dated would ever grow up and be responsible. Even though I had acted like a bohemian for quite a while, I had been trained to settle down in Middle America with a nice little house, a dog, and 2.5 kids.

Once I got to know him, I figured he had a decent line of BS. He seemed to know how to carry himself. I guess I figured we could make it work.

Oh, and plus, he was the first to ask me to marry him.

I wanted security. I was scared to death to deal with life by myself. College allowed me to live alone but not on my own. Had I been looking for security in all the wrong places?

10

"I don't want to do this," I said firmly.

"You don't *have* to do this," my aunt agreed.

"The hell she doesn't! Do you know how much money we've spent on this little party?" my father retorted.

"I *really* don't want to do this," I said again.

"Get your ass in the carriage. It's time to go," my father barked.

I felt myself back down.

"We can just go and have a really huge party," my aunt offered.

"You're just nervous," Dad said. "Let's go!"

After I downed the rest of my second screwdriver, I fixed my lipstick, tried to look happy, and got my ass in the carriage.

The horses' hooves clip clopped. They were a beautiful shade of white. I don't remember looking at my father during that ride in the carriage. I don't remember anything other than the rhythmic clopping of those white horses and how different they looked from how I felt. When we arrived, my mother was where she was supposed to be waiting for us. She was ready to accompany my father and me down the aisle to my groom.

It was a gorgeous evening in July. It wasn't too hot or muggy. The day was perfect actually—perfect in every way except for that nagging feeling in the pit of my stomach. I wanted to give into that feeling. But it was the feeling my father told me to ignore.

As we stood at the end of that long aisle, I looked up. The flowers were just as they were supposed to look— the ones in baskets and vases and the ones scattered along where I was just about to walk. The bridesmaids and groomsmen were all in their spots as planned and looked stunning. It was as if they were straight out of a bridal magazine in their black outfits and expensive bouquets and corsages.

The reverend smiled and my groom was already crying. I snapped back to reality as I watched the ring bearer trip on the white runner, sending the rings flying. Everyone told me the ring bearer was not to carry the actual rings but just fake ones. I, however, didn't listen to everyone and the ring bearer had the real rings.

There go the rings, a voice in my head said. *Are you getting this yet? Hello? I wouldn't do this if I were you.*

People laughed while he scrambled to gather the rings up again. Appearances, obligations, and distractions keep us from following the intentions we once had for our lives.

The ring bearer retrieved the rings, and everyone settled down. It was time for my parents to walk me down the aisle to begin my new life. Or was it to end my past life?

Why did I want to get married? Was it love? Was I expecting something from him? Was I running away from my past? What kind of expectations was I putting on another human?

Can he save me from myself? I wondered.

11

On the outside, I appeared to have it all together. I was determined, somewhat attractive, and focused. I was a college graduate. I set goals and always achieved them. My parents, no matter what, always put hard work at the top of their priorities. They both got up early every morning. My father went to work. My mother made our lunches and always had breakfast on the table for us before we went to school. I got my work ethic from them.

I worked my way up from a job that paid five dollars an hour to a well-paying career. I had the car (and the payment), the suits, and the right shoes, as well as the credit card debt. I knew the right people and how to deal with them. I was successful by most standards, but

I had absorbed myself into my work because I was so unhappy and was doing it because everyone seemed to expect it of me. I didn't do it because I wanted to.

My life was a lie. I did not have it all together, and I was not happy. I was running from a past I couldn't escape, and I wanted a do-over.

At exactly the same time I was getting married, I figured out it wasn't the way to get my do-over. Marriage wouldn't fix it. Unfortunately, neither of us picked the right person to marry. I was riddled with scars and oblivious to what I was doing. He wanted something I would never be able to fulfill.

It was about that same time that I began having a recurring nightmare. It continued for years.

I was in the backseat of a car that had no driver. The car changed with every dream. Sometimes I was in a semi, other times it was a car, my dad's dump truck, a regular truck, a snowplow and so on; you get the picture. The seasons changed and the time of day, but the one constant was that I was always in the backseat, and no matter what I did I was unable to gain control of the vehicle. It was frightening. I struggled every time to get into the driver's seat. I would reach for the steering wheel, but it was always just out of reach. I was always just about to crash. Nothing I did put me in that front seat. I remember the agony and frustration I felt. I often woke up sweating and in a panic, unable to fall back asleep.

Why would I agree to a marriage knowing full well how wrong it felt? I wanted my dad to tell me I didn't have to go through with the wedding. I longed for wise counsel. I needed someone to say, "It's okay, Danene. You don't have to marry him."

My aunt and my best friend tried, but my father's voice was the one I needed to hear in that moment. He needed to tell me it was okay for me to change my mind. I needed that reassurance from him.

I had run my life that way up to that moment. I made impulsive choices instead of thoughtful ones. My life ran me instead of the other way around. I was too insecure to make a decision for myself.

In 1 Corinthians 13:11, it states, "When I was a child, I spoke like a child, I thought like a child, I reasoned like a child. When I became a man, I gave up childish ways."

At what point was I going to give up my childish ways?

Not even two years into my marriage, I had an affair. He made me feel something unlike all the others. I knew him from earlier in my life, and at one point I thought I had loved him. He had cast me aside, but I thought I could get him back.

I needed something I wasn't getting in my marriage. I longed for more.

So, I flew back to my hometown for a week. I sought out this old boyfriend, slept with him, and left the next day. It ate at me. I felt like I had to tell my husband the truth. One time, the words nearly spilled out of my mouth, but I caught them. I never did tell him.

Then, I found out I was pregnant.

12

So many thoughts bounced around in my head as I sat in the Planned Parenthood office.

How did I let this happen? Could this be the other man's child? Seriously, God, why now?

The nurse came out and smiled at me. I guess she figured since I was married that the news was good.

"Congratulations! You're pregnant!" she said.

That word "pregnant" bounced around over and over in my head.

Once I got back in my car, I wanted to get as far away from my life as I could. If I left right then and drove straight back to Michigan, and never said a word, my husband would never know. I'd raise the baby alone.

I wanted to do so much in that moment but instead, I threw up. Then I drove back to my office, brushed my teeth, and called my husband. He was so excited. He brought me tulips and over the following weeks he couldn't stop showering me with affection. I hated it.

He had no idea I had already been to see a lawyer, but there was a twenty-four-month waiting period for a divorce in North Carolina—even without a child. On top of that, you have to prove a breakdown in marital relations. So, I was either going to have to rat myself out or prove that he was doing something irreconcilable.

I felt like I had no options.

We originally moved to North Carolina because of my job with a national publisher. I made good money and had great benefits. My husband, on the other hand, often got a job, lost the job, then stayed unemployed until I freaked out. He would get another job, lose it, and the pattern continued. My life did not pan out like I had thought. It was, however, going as I should have figured it would.

My focus changed and I was determined to get back to Michigan. I think fear made way for my determination. I was scared, but I was also miserable. I had to do whatever it took to get back home so I could get a divorce in a state that had a rational waiting period.

I don't think my husband had a clue when I started putting my plan together. I always wanted control.

I sat on the couch, looking through the sliding glass door out toward the little gully past our porch, when something very large seemed to loom. We lived one block in from two major interstate highways, so it was a busy section of Charlotte. It was early evening and the sun was low in the orange-and-pink-painted sky. I saw its shadow first. Then the largest owl I had ever seen landed on the power line straight across the yard from my door. Its back was toward me. Just as I was deciding to move back to Michigan, the owl gave a hoot and turned its head to look straight at me.

I didn't blink. I didn't breathe. I didn't move until the owl did. Every nerve in my body froze. I remembered my college roommate told me something about when an owl crosses your path. It is said that owls are the bringer of wisdom:

> The all-seeing owl possesses supernatural qualities and is often associated with intuition ... The owl's energy is at its peak in the very heart of darkness. When we are plunged into blindness and disorientation. He penetrates the

darkness of the blackest night. Seeing and hearing that which others cannot.

If the owl is calling you, or you are aware of the owl being present in your life, dreaming or waking, you are being called upon to open your eyes, ears and mind to the truth of a situation. To listen to the wisdom deep in your heart and soul. That still small voice is trying to reach you in some way. To assist you or help you in a current challenge you may be facing.[2]

Not the "truth of a situation" as I wanted it to be or as I wished it to be, but as it was. That still, small voice tried to reach me in my blindness and disorientation.

That night on the couch, I didn't know much about owls. I only remembered a little of what my roommate told me. Yet something stirred in my heart and reaffirmed my thought that I needed to make a change. Maybe because I was so hardheaded, I needed that kind of hit to push me in the right direction. Lord knows I hadn't found it on my own before.

I took the owl as a sign. It was time to head back to Michigan.

Have you ever been called upon to open your eyes, ears, and mind to the truth of a situation?

13

"You're doing just fine," the doctor said. "We're almost there. Take a deep breath. On the count of ten, push with everything you have, and we should be done."

A few moments later, the doctor said, "It's a girl!" as he flopped her onto my stomach.

My husband quickly agreed to cut the cord. My daughter was whisked away from me so fast that I barely had time to see her. "Is she okay?" I asked anyone who would listen.

"She's perfect!" a nurse yelled back over her shoulder.

It felt like an eternity until a nurse brought my daughter back to me. I opened the blanket they had tightly wrapped around her. I needed to make sure she had everything she was supposed to have. She flinched and squirmed. She didn't seem to like it.

Yup, ten fingers and ten toes…wait, a red birthmark? She had the most beautiful blue eyes I had *ever seen.*

I looked at my husband, who was hovering over my shoulder. "I love you!" he said. Then he kissed me.

"I love you, too," I said. I wanted to mean it.

My daughter turned her perfectly shaped head and looked right at me. "She recognizes my voice!" I said.

The doctors and nurses still worked around me, but I barely noticed. I was mesmerized by the little person in my arms. I couldn't believe how beautiful she was.

As I struggled to wrap her back up, the doctor said something about my placenta not birthing the way it was supposed to.

I didn't feel right. Something was wrong.

I felt sick to my stomach.

My husband took our daughter without saying a word. I saw my mom in the corner of the room. She didn't look well either. I told the doctor that he needed to get her out of the room.

I didn't know where my husband went. My mom held my daughter.

"The room is filling up with stars!" I moaned. I felt lightheaded. The doctor yelled orders, but everything sounded fuzzy. And I could barely see.

They strapped me down and wheeled me out. My feet were in the air and my head near the floor. The doctor was hunched over me, his mouth next to my ear. He said something, but it sounded like he was a million miles away. I didn't understand a word. Someone punched the automatic door opener and we crashed through doors like they did in episodes of *ER*.

I remember getting wheeled into a room with bright round lights over my head. Someone put a mask over my face, and everything went black.

14

lack is not a comforting color. For me it signifies
emptiness and cold, dark solitude. Nothingness.
No one. Empty. God isn't in the darkness. God is
in the light. God *is* light, isn't he? But there was no light
where I was, only darkness.

The darkness felt like an eternity and a single
moment all at the same time. I was by myself. I saw
nothing. I felt nothing tangible. I was lucid and could
hear my own thoughts and feel the emotions of each
one of those thoughts. I had a million thoughts all at
once, but I understood each one and I felt completely
overwhelmed. It was like I was in a huge, empty, pitch-
black room and my thoughts bounced around me. My
thoughts were the only thing present. Like they were

never going to end. It seemed as if during that eternity/moment, I was walking around (but I wasn't really walking), reaching out my hands, looking for something. If I was reaching for God at that time, God didn't reach back.

Matthew 8:12 basically says that people who think they know God but really don't will be "thrown into outer darkness." I felt like I was searching in that outer darkness, fumbling around like a blind person with my arms outstretched in front of me and frantically searching for something to grab hold of. But I was left with only myself and my thoughts.

That may not be the case at all, but it is how I know best to describe it now. I can tell you for sure that being left alone for that time in outer darkness, with nothing but black and my own thoughts, was truly hell for me.

Maybe it was *my* hell.

Maybe my thoughts were my god.

When I was young, my mom took my brother and me to church almost every week. I remember whining about having to go one particular week and my dad chimed in, asking why we couldn't take a day off. My mom piped up and said, "God never takes a day off from us."

So, I grew up believing there was a "God," whatever "God" was. But I drifted from the church while I was in high school. I didn't find the Bible or church relevant, and while I was in college, I told my mother that the Bible was just a book—a beautiful book of poetry and stories, but that's all it was.

I lived life on my own. I didn't care much about God. I sure didn't want his morality and rules. I guess you could say I asked God to leave me alone, and God did.

15

Everything was still dark, but I could hear my doctor's voice in my ear. "I'm going to let your husband into the recovery room now, but he isn't supposed to be in here. Do you understand?"

I wasn't sure what he was asking. I understood what he was saying, but did he mean something else? I think I nodded my head. I couldn't speak or see.

"Our daughter is beautiful, Danene. She has my eyes and your nose," my husband whispered in my ear. "You have to hold on. You've got to fight."

What was it I was fighting for?

"You can do this. I know you're going to be okay," he said.

What was he talking about?

And then he was gone.

"You're hurting me!" I yelled. Someone was literally beating on my arm.

"I'm sorry, honey. I didn't mean to hurt you," a nurse said. "I'm trying to get a vein up."

There was a sharp pain in my neck, and I was out—again.

"Push on her stomach!" came the voice of my doctor from somewhere in the room. "The last time I did I got a blood clot out the size of a Frisbee!"

He obviously had no idea I was conscious.

Phewfff, poooo, phewfff, poooo!

What was that noise? My back tooth hurt. I tried to lift my arm to feel what it was but couldn't. So, I worked with my tongue until I flipped it out from behind my tooth. Then I realized it went all the way down my throat. I couldn't breathe. I felt like I was suffocating. I was on a ventilator, and that's what was making the noise! Fighting to breath on my own, I began to vomit.

"She's aspirating!" someone screamed from across the room.

All at once I was surrounded by people. Someone turned my head to the side. I was choking. I continued to vomit. My head fell backward, and I could feel the tube sliding up my esophagus and out of my mouth.

My throat hurt, which made it painful to vomit but I couldn't stop. I was so exhausted. The room went black.

16

"Hi! We thought we'd bring your daughter to you," a nurse said. "You need to bond. It's important in these first few days."

That was my first memory post surgeries. I had two that night.

She set my daughter down on the bed next to me, her head right up to my neck. She seemed to snuggle into me. The wires and tubes running in and out of me prevented me from holding my newborn baby. All the drugs they had me on did nothing to help me connect with her either.

I believe my daughter was two days old by the time I got to see her after surgery. It was not until she was four days old that I was able to hold her in my arms.

I often wondered what effect those first days had on her. What went on in her head when she was whisked away from me—the only person she had been completely connected to for over nine months. I just knew that whatever it was, it couldn't be good.

I don't blame anyone. I know it was no one's fault. I still wonder, however, why it happened the way it did.

17

"How are we feeling today?"

One of the crew of physicians who worked on me had just breezed in, grabbing my toe with the oxygen meter on it.

"I'm not sure," I paused. "About you, but I'm having a hard time breathing." It was difficult to catch my breath. I had to take a deep breath between almost every word. I was on my fifth day in the hospital. The doctor studied my chart, checked my pulse, felt different parts of my body, and overall, looked puzzled.

"How much blood does a body hold?" I asked.

He looked up from what he was doing. "About eight to ten pints."

"How much blood did I receive during my transfusions?" I wanted to know how much blood I lost.

"You received about ten pints of blood and six pints of plasma." He was back to reading my charts.

"So basically, it's like I've been in for my 100,000-mile checkup and all my fluids have been replaced. So, I should be good for another 100,000, right?"

He smiled and shook his head in disbelief. "That's a great way to look at it. I wish all my patients had your sense of humor. Honestly, I can't believe it after all you've been through."

I had yet to hear all I'd been through. My obstetrician said we would have coffee someday and he would tell me everything that happened. He said now was not the time and that they'd given me something so I wouldn't remember. I guess they do that with some surgeries.

As the doctor flipped through the pages of my ever-thickening chart, he said he would be back in a minute. He returned with orderlies saying something about my heart and that we needed to do more tests.

Once again, I was headed down a long hallway, but we moved at a considerably slower pace this time. We entered a room with bright, round lights and they covered my face with something.

"You're going to feel as if you can't breathe, but don't worry, we won't let you suffocate." They placed a large mask over my nose and mouth and secured it in place.

"We're only going to allow a certain amount of oxygen in the mask for this test. You may feel like you're not getting enough air, but you are. We make sure of that. We need you to get comfortable and get ready. Once we start this test, we can't stop until it's done, okay?"

I nodded, doubting it would be too much. I just wanted it all to be over.

It was too much. It was the worst battery of tests I had ever been through. I thought I was suffocating. In fact, I *knew* I was suffocating. Right there, right then, on that table, I thought I was going to die!

After the tests, I was rolled back out into the hall. Orderlies were supposed to come back and get me in a minute.

That was one *long* minute. It felt more like an hour.

I lay there in my hospital gown, freezing, exhausted, filthy, and bloated. I was sixty-four pounds over my normal weight. My hormones raged, and I began to cry. With nothing but my gown to dry my eyes or my nose, I lay in that hallway crying.

Wasn't this supposed to be the happiest time of my life? I was supposed to come in, have a baby, and go home. This wasn't part of the plan.

"Your life was spared, Danene," said a gentle, soothing, confident voice.

I turned to see who was there. No one.

Frustrated and embarrassed at what I must look like, I shifted around on the gurney. As I settled back in, I heard, "You would have died living only a life of self-fulfillment five days ago," the voice finished.

There was neither judgment nor condemnation. It was just stated as a fact. I couldn't see anyone, yet what was said was very clear, very strong. There was no denying the words spoken.

"Living only a life of self-fulfillment" continued to ring in my ears, and my life hit another point of no return. I survived against all odds, according to my doctors.

What did that mean? Why me? Why did I get a second chance to live a life that is more than mere self-fulfillment?

Maybe I wouldn't have heard that pivotal teaching anywhere but in that cold, lonely hallway after everything I had been through. I was beaten down. It was the first time in a long time that I knew I couldn't do it on my own. I had no control over my situation. This time

I *really* needed something more. I needed doctors and nurses to save my life. I needed other people to care for my newborn child. Hell, I needed other people just to get out of bed!

I had no control. For a control freak like me, that was way more than a humbling experience.

Maybe that's what it took for me to realize God was pursuing me. God wanted more for my life. And in the silence, I heard those words. God told me I came back from death.

Maybe God does want that none shall perish?

18

had eight ultrasounds before giving birth to my daughter. At first, they weren't sure what was happening. Around six months, my doctor thought I was suffering from placenta previa, which is when the placenta is over the cervix and would come out before I gave birth to my daughter. The doctor was worried about that.

A month later, he decided my placenta moved enough that it was no longer a concern. They continued to monitor the situation and told me I was progressing normally.

My due date was set for October 30. It came and went. I experienced a few labor pains but nothing substantial. It was clear I wasn't going to have the baby on time. I agreed with my doctor to let labor happen at its own pace. However, by mid-November—eleven months after my affair—my doctor thought I should be induced the next Monday.

We've already covered that part of the story.

You're probably wondering why the room filled up with stars and all the rest. As it turned out, I had a placenta accrete, which is when the placenta attaches itself to—and in my case, nearly through—the uterine wall. At least that's how I understood it. The placenta acted kind of like a tumor. Because of that, the placenta will not birth. If it is pulled on, it can tear. If the placenta tears, it bleeds. A placenta has an artery and two veins connected to it, so it bleeds profusely. Hence, my lack of oxygen and why I saw stars.

I know I had two surgeries that night. A perinatal specialist was able to do the surgeries inside me, so I have no external scars. I know the second time they operated, they did so in the recovery room because they didn't have time to get me to the operating room. At one point my heart stopped, my kidneys shut down, and I flatlined. I wonder now if that happened when the nurse beat on my arm when she was unable to find a vein. I don't know what they did to get my heart pumping again, and I am not sure how long it lasted. I assume that's when I went on the ventilator. Since they were unable to get a vein due to the loss of blood, they put a port in my neck. I remember that. I still have the scars.

I woke up in the intensive care unit with the uncomfortable port in my neck, an eighteen-shooter IV in my left arm, which was strapped down, and an EKG monitored my heart. That was when my lactation specialist rolled in the dual breast pump machine. I burst into tears when I looked at the contraption. That saying "death warmed over" was how I felt. I could not get my bloated, aching, hooked-up, and strung-out body to the side of the bed and hoist my boobs up into that machine, only to throw every ounce of milk away because my milk was laced with morphine!

My mother knew exactly what I thought. I didn't have to say a word. She got up, hauled the machine out of the room, and explained that while she knew I said I wanted to breast feed my baby, circumstances had changed a bit and that was no longer the plan. Then my mom came back into the room and told me she raised my brother and me on formula, and we turned out just fine. She knew exactly what to say.

The intensive care unit was an interesting place. I had a suicidal man next to me my second night. I remember lying there, barely able to move, and having to listen to him say over and over again, "I just want to die! Why can't you just let me end it? Why didn't you let me die?"

I thought to myself, *I'm just about ready to come on over there and kill you myself!* Stay with me for a second. I was fighting to live, had just given birth to a baby who needed me, and they put *that* guy next to me? At the time, I wasn't thinking about what pain that man must have been in to want to end his life. I think the worst part is that he had no hope for a brighter tomorrow.

While I was in intensive care, I learned that one of the nurses on shift when I had my daughter had called into a national radio show to ask people to pray for me and my newborn. I had no idea the severity of my situation at that point.

After the intensive care unit, I moved to high risk. I wasn't able to move to the maternity floor. I found out later that was actually a good thing because I didn't have roommates. Then my doctor learned I had congestive heart failure. I assume it was from all the fluids they pumped into me. That's what landed me in the cold, lonely hallway. Afterward, I was referred to as "the miracle patient."

I also remember that the black void scared the hell out of me! It felt real. If there was an eternity, I didn't want to spend it that way.

I continued to wonder if all those prayers made a difference and if it was God who said I was "living only a life of self-fulfillment." Did that lead to my outer darkness? I was a pretty selfish person.

At any cost, I pursued my comfort and pleasure. I didn't care about anyone else. I never thought about anyone else. I gave birth to a beautiful, fragile life, yet I continued to live as if life was all about me. It made sense that my behavior would lead to outer darkness.

The whole situation was difficult to comprehend, yet, in that hallway, I felt a tiny flame ignite inside me. I wondered if it was time to unravel the mystery of why *my* life—my selfish, self-fulfilling, pleasure-seeking life—was spared. Did I really hear those words? I really *heard* them. And they affected me.

Could I change?

It seemed too big of a responsibility to ignore.

19

asked myself if I could change. After everything that happened, it should have been easy for me to get on the right track. It seemed like a good course of action. The problem was, I really didn't change that much. I believed my team of doctors when they told me how close I got to not leaving the hospital. I felt the physical effects of everything that happened to me—the blood transfusions, operations, damage to my pituitary gland, the extra pounds I had gained from flooding my system with fluids, the congestive heart failure. I knew my situation was real.

I knew my father, who had not planned on being in North Carolina for my daughter's birth, took a last minute, middle-of-the-night flight to get to me before it was too late. My father-in-law came as well. I was told the priest wanted to give me last rites, but since I wasn't Catholic, that never happened. I knew how close I had come. I *knew* my life was spared. I heard that voice in the hallway.

After the novelty and my gratefulness wore off, however, I went back to my same reckless behavior. My marriage quickly disintegrated. And I found my way back to my destructive path. I went right back to the same selfish person I thought I'd given up in that cold, lonely hallway.

On the one hand, I knew I had to put my old self behind me and learn to give and compromise. On the other hand, however, I realized how short life was and how everything could change in the blink of an eye. I could have a baby and not wake up. I could be involved in a fatal accident. I could have a doctor tell me I had six months to live.

My situation had not improved. I knew how ill-suited my husband and I were for each other. I knew how miserable we made each other. And I knew how hostile that environment would be for our daughter.

Our arguments turned physical. That was how we sought control when screaming and swearing weren't enough. If something didn't change, was I really supposed to live out my days like that? We were two hurting people who continued to hurt each other.

I wasn't sure what I was supposed to learn. Should I stay or go? Should I stick with my marriage or move on?

20

My husband continued to drift in and out of jobs. As soon as my maternity leave was over, I went back to work and back to being the breadwinner. Even with all my health complications, I went back to work a few weeks early. Someone had to make money and pay the bills! We had a child to feed. We had to buy diapers and clothes for her. Besides that, staying in that house with my husband twenty-four hours a day was not good for my health. We could not stop fighting. A week after I got out of the hospital, we got into a shoving match that nearly landed me back in the hospital because I started hemorrhaging. My parents were staying with us, and my mother begged me to leave him.

That wasn't how it was supposed to be. What happened to my happily ever after? Where was my Prince Charming?

I was robbed of getting to be a mom because I had to play dad, too. I had to put food on the table and make sure our electricity stayed on. I had to make sure housework got done and the snow got shoveled from the driveway. That was not how it was supposed to happen. That wasn't what I signed up for. That wasn't the way I grew up. I didn't want to be the dad. I wanted to be the mom. I wanted to stay home with my child and be the caregiver. My mom ran the house and raised my brother and me. My father's responsibility was to support our family. This was not at all how my marriage worked. I hated my husband for that. I hated that he couldn't man up. Someone had to, and I was beyond angry that it was me.

My frustration continued to grow.

Many times I thought, *If I have to do this on my own, I may as well lighten the load by one mouth.*

Lighten the load! That's what I was thinking as I stood between the living and dining rooms of our small apartment in Farmington, Michigan. I was wearing a dark-blue double-breasted suit and heels. I waited for him to come home from his morning coffee and paper run.

I looked at my watch. He was going to make me late for work again. Plus, he never even brought me coffee. I walked over to the phone. "I'm not going to be into work today," I told my boss. "There's something I need to take care of."

That day, I started the process to fulfill the reason I had moved back to Michigan to begin with. I tried to save my marriage as best as a selfish, self-absorbed, albeit, good-intentioned person could, but it was broken and beyond fixing.

21

"You have to concede on some things, Danene. You can't have it all," my lawyer said. "That's not how divorce works," she said, as we struggled to find compromise.

To be honest, that's not how any of this was supposed to work. I was supposed to get married and live happily ever after. When that failed, I was supposed to ask for a divorce. My husband was supposed to agree. We would be civil, if not friendly. We were going to be mature. We were going to work our new chapter out. Everyone was going to be better off. It was supposed to be over quickly, then we would move on with our lives. Divorce was supposed to be a blip on our radar and then it would be done.

Our daughter would be unaffected by her parent's divorce.

"If you want this over with, you're going to have to give in a bit," my lawyer kept telling me.

My anger with the legal system continued to mount, and I thought about taking matters into my own hands. I even thought about killing my husband on more than one occasion. I could see myself walking straight up to him and strangling him with my bare hands. I could rationalize why it would be okay to pull out a gun and blow his head off. I imagined the gun in my hand and how the cold steel would feel as I fired off a bullet. I imagined the blood soaking my hands and my shirt, splattering all over my face. I imagined the relief I would feel.

I can truly understand why some people go completely crazy during custody battles. I don't condone it, but I do understand. I was there. I am not any more rational or mentally stable than anyone else.

I just never purchased the gun.

I think if I had gone to the extent of purchasing a gun, I may have gone through with it. I hated my husband that much. If I had more money, I may have run with our daughter. I was *that* selfish. Anyone who has been through a custody battle knows what I'm talking about. You have expectations when you start divorce proceedings. Then your expectations get blown out of the water. Like a hand grenade tossed into the middle of it all, destruction abounds, and the shrapnel hits everyone in its path. It's bloody, it's messy, and it hurts everyone.

I didn't want to concede. The court would have to force me to concede. I wanted it all, and I thought I should have it. Hell, I worked for it all! And I was the better parent. I had the good job, the health insurance, and the rational mind. Me!

Wait, was that what it was still all about?

22

tanding with the refrigerator door wide open, I half expected something to jump out at me. My phone rang. I grabbed it off the receiver.

"Hello?"

"Hi, Danene, are you sitting?" It was an ex-boyfriend from college. He lived just up the block from me.

I looked around for a chair. None were close enough, so I leaned against the counter and braced myself.

"What's going on?" I asked.

"Gilly's been in a terrible accident," he said. "He was on 275. I guess his car broke down. He was outside trying to fix it or something and someone hit him. Danene, it's bad. He's been flown to Ann Arbor via helicopter."

I slid to the floor. I don't remember hanging up the phone. I just sobbed on that kitchen floor. *Oh God. Not Gilly. Oh God, please. Not Dan.*

I had four best friends in my life. Dan was one of them. I met him my sophomore year of college. He was friends with a guy I dated. He was in the same fraternity. He and I clicked right away, but we were never more than good friends. I know I made a few of his girl-friends very nervous. They couldn't believe we could just be "friends." But we were. He never once hit on me… and I loved him for that!

I went over to his house after class one day and found him sitting in the dark. He had sunglasses on, and Roy Orbison played on his turntable. I could tell he was into the music, so I sat down and listened with him. We probably sat there for twenty minutes or so. Finally, he said, "I loved Roy before he died."

I just nodded, not quite sure what to do with that information. I looked around at all the posters and pictures he had on his walls from music magazines. He finally told me Roy Orbison had died that day, which invoked the trip down memory lane.

We sat there for another long while. Then he said, with that smile he had, "This is how you know you're really good friends. When you can sit and never say a word, and it isn't awkward." We were those friends.

It was an early spring evening the last time I saw Dan. He came to Farmington to meet my daughter. He looked good. I could tell life was going well for him. I always thought we would remain friends after school, and that night in Farmington reinforced that belief. We would stay in touch, share pictures of our children and grandchildren with each other, and spend time together. I hoped he'd marry a nice woman and that we could remain close.

Looking through tear-filled eyes at the scuffed, worn tiles of my kitchen floor, I realized none of that was going to happen. Dan had been hit by a passing car and thrown many yards into oncoming traffic on 275 outside of Detroit. He lived three days, but never came out of the coma.

His funeral had to be the largest Royal Oak, Michigan saw in a long time. I am guessing the procession from the church to the cemetery was two miles long. Once at the cemetery, his fraternity brothers all carried white roses down the aisle and placed them on his casket. More than one hundred brothers walked down that aisle to pay tribute while "Danny Boy" played on the bagpipes. It was almost more than I could bear.

I remember looking around for someone to stand with, someone to be comforted by. I didn't have real friends there though. I only saw scorned ex-boyfriends who couldn't have cared less if I was hurting.

It was even harder when they ushered us out before they closed the casket at the funeral home. They had everyone walk past his casket. I didn't want to walk past him. I did not wish to see proof that my friend was really dead. I felt pressured to do it. I barely looked at him. He was so puffy. I know people always say this, but it really didn't look like Dan. And I didn't want that to be my last memory. I can still see him in that coffin, with a strange smile and his hands folded across his chest.

23

The finalization of my divorce, in court, was three days away now. Two weeks prior, we buried Dan. As miserable as I thought my marriage was, I still felt like I was experiencing another death. The complete and utter failure of my life as I knew it should perhaps not have come as a surprise, but the finalization of it all was difficult to process. My life was status quo as long as I kept moving. When it all came to a halt, however, that was when I felt like I was grabbed by the back of the neck and had my nose shoved into my concession.

I couldn't make my marriage work. That only added to my doubting myself. My life took a turn I never saw coming.

Then my phone rang...

I wish I could describe how the phone call went and what happened, but I can't. I don't even remember who called me. I do know that's when I found out Candi, another best friend, had died in a horrible car accident in Florida.

How many breaking points could I bear? It felt like my whole world started to crumble around me. I had no foundation to stand on. What I thought of as my foundation, the good people I had surrounded myself with, had disappeared.

There must have been a few hundred people at Candi's funeral visitation. People struggled to get in the door. Candi was buried the next day, which was also the day I was to be in court to finalize my divorce.

Candi and I had been friends since ninth grade. We saw each other through tough times. Her father had been killed on the job from a downed power line when her mom was still pregnant with her. That was hard on Candi, as one can imagine. She was madly in love with a man she never got to meet.

We always had fun when we were together. She liked to laugh, joke, and be happy. Candi always smiled, she was always positive, and had a quick, cutting wit. She and I spent hours and hours talking on the phone.

We smoked for the first time together. We got it from a girl at school and then spent the night together at her house and walked to the high school to smoke it near the track and football fields. We kept asking each other, "Do you feeling anything yet?"

We stayed in touch after I went away to college. I saw her every time I went home. At some point, Candi married a military man and moved away. A few years after she got married, I called her at two in the morning. I missed her and knew it would only be ten at night in San Diego. She sleepily answered the phone.

"Hey," I started in. "You sleeping already? What are you, old?"

"It's two in the morning, Danene," Candi replied. "What are you, drunk?"

"Maybe. What do you mean it's two in the morning?" I asked. "Aren't you in San Diego?"

"No!" Then she laughed. "We moved three months ago, Ding Dong!"

"Maybe I should call more often?" I suggested.

That's the way we were. We went for periods of time where we didn't talk at all, but we always picked up where we left off. We never guilt tripped each other either.

I don't think I ever received closure for Candi's death. Having to be on the other side of the state for a divorce, when instead, I should have been burying a dear friend, has made her death especially difficult for me. I have mourned her for a long time. I always thought Candi would by my friend—a real friend—to hang around town with. My other best friend since eighth grade didn't live in the same town. In fact, she lived in my hometown of Plainwell for only two years, so even though we made a good effort to spend time together, it wasn't the same.

I lost Dan, Candi, my marriage, and many of my dreams all at once in the spring of 1997.

24

fter eighteen months, two counties, two judges, three attorneys, and way too much money, I was divorced. It bankrupted me financially and mentally, but it was done. My divorce was no blip on the radar. It was more like an annoying alarm clock I couldn't shut off or a pain that wouldn't go away no matter how much medication I took.

I have never felt such intense hatred for anyone as I did for my ex-husband. Any chance we had of any kind of post-divorce relationship was destroyed. There was no room for compromise or working together for the benefit of our daughter. It turned into a huge pissing match.

Our relationship continued to be toxic and physical between us. The court ordered us to meet at a police station when we exchanged our daughter to curtail the violence for most of our daughter's early years.

Our daughter sensed our hatred for each other. She felt the constant tension. She cried every time she was dropped off or picked up. One day, when she was about six, she told me she didn't want to go to her dad's house.

Good, finally, this nightmare can be over for us. She doesn't want to see him anymore. She's tired of being shoved off onto someone else for her caregiving when she's with him; she barely spends any time with him anyway.

When my ex-husband came to my door to pick our daughter up that weekend, I told him she didn't want to go. He demanded to see her. I lied and told him she wasn't there. As I tried to shut the door, he caught a glimpse of our daughter in the next room. My ex-husband forced the door open, which knocked me off balance. He started for my living room. I followed him. I shoved him in his chest to push him back out onto the porch. That just made him angrier. He grabbed at the screen door, nearly ripping it out of its frame. He attempted to force his way back through. I jumped between him and our daughter. He grabbed me by the arms and threw me out of the way. I hit the door and it slammed into the wall, which left a hole. Before my ex-husband could get any further into the room, I jumped in front of him again. I successfully shoved him outside. I slammed and locked the door but expected him to crash through at any moment, but nothing happened. I heard a car door slam then he drove away.

I breathed a sigh of relief. I thought it was over. I remember the terrified look on my daughter's face. My neighbor had been in the kitchen and witnessed the whole thing. I looked at my neighbor, then looked at my already bruising arms. I shook almost uncontrollably. I couldn't believe what had just happened. My neighbor thought I should call the police, but I didn't want the police involved.

Just as we began to calm down and get ourselves back together, there was a knock at the door. I was too scared to answer it. I ran to the other door to lock it. There was a police cruiser out front. I knew the officer. I went to the front door and opened it.

My ex went to the police station and reported the incident. He said I beat him up. The officer told me he was skeptical. He said he needed to get our statements. I showed him my arms. He suggested I go to the police station to get photos taken of my bruises. He was very understanding. The officer from the sheriff's department was not. I could tell he didn't believe my side of the story.

My neighbor and I did everything they asked of us, including the photos. Then, I tried to put the event behind me. I thought it was over, but several weeks later I got a call from the prosecuting attorney's office. They were pressing charges against my ex-husband. I was stunned.

He was given the chance to plea-bargain out of the charges, but he refused. They tried three times, but he probably thought he could win the case. So, it went to trial. There were six jurors. My neighbor, the police officer, my ex-husband, and I had to testify. I was on the stand for almost four hours.

My ex-husband's attorney kept at me. He tried to poke holes in my story. Later in my testimony, the lawyer said there were discrepancies in my written statement versus what I said on the stand. He asked things like, "Was it forty-five seconds or two minutes?" Then, he would follow that with, "You keep changing your story."

Once I got exasperated, I finally said to him, "I am not the one who went to the police. I am not the one who pursued charges. If I thought for one minute that I would be here on this stand, giving my testimony, I would have been much more detailed in my statement to the police. I am doing the best I can." I remember the look on the jurors' faces. I could tell they believed me.

The jury returned with a guilty verdict. When polled, at the request of my ex-husband's attorney, all six jurors said they thought my ex-husband was guilty.

The prosecuting attorney was thrilled. She wanted the maximum sentence. "We can put him in jail for ninety days!" she whispered in my ear. I remember her red lipstick was crooked and out of the lines of her lips, and there was some on her left front tooth as she spoke. She seemed like the enemy. She wasn't, she fought hard for me. But I didn't want my ex-husband to go to jail. That was never my intent. When I decided to divorce my ex-husband, I only wanted us to not be married. Why couldn't we do that with peace?

In the weeks after the incident but before the trial, my daughter and I talked about why she didn't want to go with her dad. She said it was because he never spent time with her.

So, when the judge asked why I didn't want him receiving the maximum sentence, I asked if I could speak freely. He nodded and asked me to step to the microphone.

I explained the conversation I had with my daughter. She had spoken out of frustration because her dad dropped her off at her grandparents and friends instead of spending time with her. I longed for a mature relationship with my ex-husband where we put our daughter's needs first.

I think my attorney was angry, but I didn't care. Thankfully, I began to realize that our long-term relationship was more important than revenge. Putting him in jail for ninety days wouldn't solve anything. In reality, a jail sentence had the potential to make things worse.

It was important that my ex-husband was charged and found guilty *before* I let it go. There was no doubt I had my lessons to learn, but that lesson was for him. He crossed a line. I appreciate my attorney for stepping in and reintroducing normal. I let my ex-husband get away with too much to try to get along and not cause waves. Keeping him placated was very important to me. He could make my life hell, but I let things escalate too far. I let him get away with too much. So, it was important for me to have that kind of closure. Sometimes we can get in the way of other people's life lessons. I finally learned to make things about my daughter and less about me.

"How many times must I forgive? Seven?"

"No," Jesus says in Matthew 18:22, "not seven but seventy times seven."

"Are you sure Jesus?"

Only if you want peace!

25

Three years after my divorce, I quit my job in sales management. I had been in that job for ten years—a third of my life at that point. I felt a real dis-ease in my soul. I was searching, again. I tried to demote myself to a sales representative position because the management schedule was too demanding for my life as a single parent. The company wouldn't allow it, so I quit. I found another sales job that required minimal overnight travel.

There's a lot of freedom that comes with being an outside sales representative. As long as you get to the office when you're supposed to and make your quotas, no one cares what you do during the workday. Many of the reps met for lunch, which often stretched into happy hour. I had a flexible daycare provider who also happened to live next door to me, so if I didn't get right home after work, all I had to do was call and she would take care of my daughter. It's not like I did it all the time, but I still wasn't used to my role as a mother. I found meaning and satisfaction in my job.

I became close with another sales representative. Our offices were across the hallway from each other. I liked everyone in our office, but he was especially charming. He was not a handsome man, but certainly made up for it with his easygoing demeanor and wit. I always enjoyed being around people who can make me laugh. He was a consummate salesperson and offered good advice. I was grateful for his help.

He often made comments about something I wore or the color of my lipstick. Thinking back, I knew it wasn't innocent, but it made me feel good. It made me feel like a woman likes to feel—at least how *this* woman liked to feel. I wasn't interested in a relationship, so I didn't think much about it.

He was always a gentleman when the reps met for lunch or happy hour. He was the guy who stood when one of the women got up to go to the restroom. He was the one to pull out our chairs for us, help us with our jackets, and open the doors for us. At some point he began sitting next to me at every meeting and every lunch. I liked the attention. I knew he had a child from a previous relationship, but so did I. He didn't offer much information and I didn't ask questions.

I began to get restless. It had been a long time. I had gotten used to getting sex when I wanted or needed it. It still had nothing to do with love. It was merely a physical release for me. I did a good job keeping my emotions out of it—no one broke through the wall.

We began regularly meeting to smoke a joint and get a drink. We had a couple other friends who occasionally joined us but often it was just the two of us. Our conversations turned quite flirtatious and neither one of us tried to keep it clean.

One day, we met at a busy corner bar and grill. I was dressed to conquer and after a few drinks I brazenly looked him dead in the eyes and invited him back to my place. I still remember the look on his face—utter shock and absolute disbelief. He had worked hard for it and wanted it for so long, but he couldn't believe what he heard. I held the cards. Whether we got together or not was my choice.

Men will always go as far as you let them, and I was ready to let him. I remember the anticipation as we drove to my house that afternoon. It was a high I didn't need any drugs to achieve. I felt powerful and in charge.

It wasn't until the sweat dripped off his nose and hit my face that I realized what I was really doing, and it made me sick to my stomach.

26

What is control? Is it consuming and manipulating everything within your power or is it restraint despite the ability to use and manipulate all that's around you? Do we even have control or simply the *illusion* of it?[3]

Using people fulfilled that illusion of control for me. At the time, it made me feel powerful. I thought I had it all together because I had control. I believed that made me attractive—for a while. I never let anyone too close. If someone got too close, they would be able to see my cracks, flaws, and vulnerability. I hated those things, especially vulnerability. It made me feel weak. The *real* me was so different from the facade I meticulously constructed. If they got through my walls, they might not like what they found. The pulled-together woman I presented to the world was actually a mess. She was needy and codependent. She was desperate for someone—anyone—to love her despite her many flaws.

I didn't want anyone close. Eventually, they all left anyway. So, I learned that if I kept people at a distance, if I put myself into relationships with no real commitment, then no one could leave me.

I've heard it said that sinning is like being burned by a hot iron.[4] The first time it touches your skin it hurts for quite some time. After a few days, the sting goes away though, and all that remains is tougher, calloused skin. If you burn yourself in the same way again, that layer is impervious to the same pain. It has been forever altered.

Back to my relationship, I was tough and callous. I knew I was doing the wrong thing. I knew he was married before I ever slept with him. I just didn't care. After a while, I no longer felt that same pang of conscience. My needs were being met and that was all I focused on. That was all sex meant to me then—a physical need.

In the beginning, it was someone else's needs being met, but quickly it became all about my needs. That is the truth. I have learned we do not heal or change until we look the truth straight in the eye and deal with it. Vulnerability and all.

Our affair lasted more than a year and a half. The last few months, we became emotionally and physically abusive. He wanted to control me and possess me, but I resisted.

He followed me when I went out of town for work. We often became violent, especially after we started drinking on those trips. I am sure my peers heard us. They all acted as if nothing had gone on the night before. Only once was I asked about bruising on my thumb and hand.

His wife was unable to cope with the news of the affair, so she moved out. He decided he wanted to buy me an engagement ring, saying he wanted to marry me. But I never saw a future with him. He was just a pawn in my game of self-fulfillment. I wanted to put it down, give it up, stop returning to that well, but I couldn't. I kept going back. Proverbs 26:11 states, "Like a dog returns to its vomit, so a fool repeats their folly."

I didn't think I was worth any more than I received. I chose two similar situations in college; "dating" men who were already committed but wanted me on the side. And I continued to make the same mistakes. When we don't see or realize our intrinsic value, we allow ourselves to be sold short.

He was insanely jealous and accused me of doing all sorts of things I didn't do. As it turns out, *he* was doing those things he accused me of.

I'll never forget the last time I saw him. I had broken it off between us a few weeks prior because I found him on my front porch listening in on my phone conversation. He wouldn't take our breakup as the end. He called me that night, and I remember hearing someone walk into his house during the call. A woman started an argument on the other end. I knew it was his wife.

"Let me talk to her!" I yelled. "Does she know you won't stop bugging me?"

He acted like he hung up the phone, but he hadn't. I don't know if that was intentional or an oversight.

"She's nothing to me," he said to the woman on his end. "She's a whore."

It felt like I got punched in the stomach. I wonder why, if I really had steeled myself against feelings, did those words hurt so?

Maybe because it was true.

Basically, I *was* a whore. I quickly became an angry, crazy, and enraged whore! Within seconds, my heart-rate jumped from resting rate to "going to explode in my chest rate." *I* had been trying to cut him off. *I* was done with him! He was stalking and calling me all the time. He sat on my front porch listening in on my conversation like a creep.

Revenge kicked in. I wanted his wife to know what had really happened. I grabbed my purse and jumped in my car. My legs shook so bad, my foot jumped off the gas pedal as I drove.

What in the world was I going to do when I got there? I wanted his wife to know what she was dealing with. I had enough of him. I put that addiction down once and for all!

When I pulled into his driveway, my legs still shaking, I took a minute to compose myself. I wasn't sure I'd be able to stand to get out of the car.

"I'll destroy your life if you destroy mine, bitch." His voice came from behind the bushes next to the garage. I suppose he saw my car pull in. Why else would he be in the bushes next to the garage?

Still shaking I kept moving. He followed behind me and repeated himself. The same man who continued to profess his love for me threatened me. Before I made it to the door, it swung open. His wife stepped out, holding a small, white dog.

"He's crazy," I said to her. "We were having an affair, but I broke it off with him a while ago! And now, he won't leave me alone! I am sick of him calling me, sick of him showing up uninvited and unannounced at my home—where my daughter lives—and I just want you to know what kind of a man you're really dealing with."

Satisfied, I turned and headed back toward my car. He had walked right up by her, but she had moved away from him. Halfway back to my car, no longer shaking, I turned and added, "I think you and I are smarter than this. I think we both deserve more than this guy has to offer."

With that, I confidently walked back to my car. My headlights illuminated them as they stood on the porch. She looked dumbfounded as she clung to her dog. He looked like he was going to kill me.

Saying the words "deserve more than this guy has to offer" out loud that night, might have been the first step I took in actually believing it.

Is there something you have wanted to put down, give up, stop returning to, but haven't been able to?

27

My questions are not asked
They're not important
I know the answers
I am worth little more than trash
To you, to myself

—excerpt from "The Gum Wrapper"
by Danene K. Shumaker

All those years after my second chance, something or someone else continued to run my life. It wasn't me. I wasn't running my life! I chased after my impulses—the same ones that ran me into that ditch.

I spent all that time contriving a controlled front, but I was in control of nothing. I was tired of feeling like I was running around and gaining no ground. Do you remember the people who would spin the plates on poles? They're running around in circles trying to keep all those plates spinning on top of skinny poles without crashing to the floor.

That is how I felt. I ran around, accomplishing nothing. I was tired of the facade I had built. I was exhausted and had no place to turn because I had no one to trust. Certainly not myself. I learned to not talk about my problems, not to trust anyone, and certainly not to feel anything. It was easier to manage my life that way.

If it was so much simpler, why was I exhausted and so unfulfilled?

That chapter of my life with the affair became the proverbial straw that broke the camel's back. I took a good long look at myself in the mirror and examined the person I had become. I thought about the person I had once wanted to be. I had strayed so far.

I thought about my grandmother stroking my hair while we sat on a porch swing on the banks of Lake Superior when I was just a little girl. She told me I could be anything I set my mind to. What would my grand- mother say if she knew the person I had become? Very few knew. Most people didn't really care and it's easy to hide as long as you keep up the front.

Have you heard the expression that says something to the effect of, "People don't change until the pain of not changing outweighs the pain of change?"

Maybe I could have justified it if I was happy. Instead, I was angry, defensive, frustrated, and morose. I had become a lot of things, but happy wasn't one of them. I looked in the mirror and hated the person I saw. I hated the compromises I made. I wished I could erase it all. That's what I was thinking about the night I slipped into my bathtub. I needed to cleanse and renew.

That question "Is this *all* you've set your mind to?" played on a loop in my head.

28

was a thirty-three-year-old divorced, single mother. That realization again, of my daughter and my responsibilities, slowed and quieted my racing thoughts for a moment. But when I remembered the wreck my life had become, I quickly returned to the mindset that, *she'd be better off without me.*

Who heard me, what I looked like, or how that could affect anyone else was of no consequence for me. Soon, I was sobbing so hard I didn't even make a sound. I did something without even thinking. I began to pray.

Maybe it started out as a curse. I was angry with myself, so I shouted at and blamed someone else. Jesus?

After all, praying wasn't something I did.

"Jesus. Jesus. Jesus." I kept saying His name over and over again. I rocked back and forth, holding my knees to my chest, sobbing, snot still hanging. I don't know how many times I said His name, but the now-cold water nearly spilled onto the bathroom floor. Yet, I continued.

"I've run my life off in a ditch. I'm a mess and I don't know what to do," I said aloud. "I gotta give this up—this way of life—these problems. I have to give it all up. I can't do this anymore! I can't live like this any longer. I give up! I surrender! Is that what you want to hear? I've tried everything else! There *has* to be something more than me! If you're real, take this from me!"

No longer crying, I heard the water from the bathtub running again. I felt the cold water coming from the showerhead. I should have been freezing cold, but instead I was warm and totally calm. I felt light, if that makes sense. I had felt so, so heavy before.

I remember looking around in the shower. I shut off the water. The warmth I felt started in my heart. It radiated outward, through my chest, up into my head and down through my arms and legs. It felt like the warmth wrapped itself around me. I felt at peace for the first time in years. I had none of the feelings that led me to the bath that night. They were gone.

I wish you could feel what I felt. My prayer was long, and I confessed a lot of things that made me hate myself. I thought if anyone else heard those things about me, they wouldn't love me anymore. But it felt like I had a conversation with Jesus, and I told him everything. His response was love and absolute acceptance.

In that moment, I *knew* Jesus was for real. Real like the book you hold in your hands. Real like a sunset or the wind blowing through your hair. Real. And I felt like a new flower pushing through the dirt in spring.[5] I knew I was given a sign—a gift. I didn't have any idea what it meant. But I knew it was time to get moving. I didn't yet know what the next step would be, but I knew I could take it.

Why was God so insistent on reaching *me*?

29

one of it made sense. I always believed God existed. As a child, I sat in a chaise lounge by our pool at night and looked up at the stars for long stretches of time. It made me feel uniquely special and totally insignificant all at the same time. I remember thinking how small our planet was, even in the scheme of only what I could fathom in our night sky. That made me feel very insignificant. Yet scientists have found no other life forms?

Why not any other life forms but us? That made me feel special. Like the universe was too huge to have just happened. We are too unique. That's amazing, at least it was to me.

But Jesus? As in virgin birth, sinless man, and Son of God, Jesus? *That* didn't make any sense to me.

Then I gave up my right to myself.

I surrendered my natural independence and my self-will.

> "This is where the battle has to be fought. The things that are right, noble, and good from the natural standpoint are the very things that keep us from being God's best."[6]

With all those self-help books I read, I still wasn't able to help myself. What I mean is that the more I concentrated and worked on myself, the less I could see. I continued to be so focused on me, I couldn't see anyone else. Some would say I had given a foothold to the devil. And *that* is what I had to give up.

We want to think, and we want others to think, that we have it all together. That somehow, we could learn enough. Most of us seem to believe that we are supposed to "pull ourselves up by our bootstraps." That way, we don't appear as if we need help.

I found the opposite to be true.

Is this another example of why Jesus is so countercultural?

I gave *me* up! I knew I needed help. I remember surrendering to Jesus. I can still go back to the exact moment and feel that same deep-seated need to *give up myself.*

Listen to me: my selfishness, my expectations, my perceived control of my environment and the people in it, my agenda. Is any of this resonating? I needed to surrender all of that for my life to become something greater than what I had set my mind to.

Do you think God takes the time to speak directly into our lives? And if so, do you listen? And perhaps most important, do you keep listening?

30

ithin a year of meeting Jesus in my bathtub, I became familiar with a story in the Bible. The story is of a woman at a well. The very first time I read the story, I was amazed at the depth of feelings I experienced. For me, it became living word. Each time I read that story, a new and different nuance came out. I say to my friends that scripture is like a diamond, with so many facets and angles and dispersion of light. I'd like to try to give you a look at how I saw the story relating to my life. It may help you to understand that I now see much of the Bible as metaphorical—God using stories to speak truth into our lives.

The Woman at the Well – Danene's Story

Jesus was worn out from a long trip, so He sat down near a well while his friends and students went into town to get food. It was around noon. A woman came to get water from that well. She most likely was an outcast from society or an introvert. Otherwise, she would have come with all the other women. Coming to the well was a social event back in those days, a time to see your friends. Yet, she chose to go when she thought no one else would be around.

But Jesus was around.

He asked the woman for some water. She questioned why He was even speaking to her. Jews didn't speak to people from her country of Samaria. Their rivalry was well known throughout the Middle East.

"If you understood the generosity of God and who I am," Jesus replied as told in John 4:10, "you would be asking *me* for a drink and I would give *you* fresh, *living* water."

"You don't even have a bucket, and this well is deep." Now she could have meant just that. The well was deep.

What if she meant something else? What if she meant something more like, "You have no idea the depths I have gone to, and I am past the point of redemption." Think of the depths of human nature, of human life, think of the depths of the "wells" in you.

"How would *you* be able to give *me* a drink?" she asked.

Jesus showed her that the water of what was called Jacob's well yielded very short satisfaction. Of whatever waters of comfort we drink, we shall thirst again.[7]

Jesus says to her, "Everyone who drinks this water will get thirsty again and again. But anyone who drinks the water I give will never thirst."

Maybe Jesus *does* have water that He can give that will make it so you never thirst again. But God created these bodies to need sixty ounces of water every day. So, it seems certain that everyone will thirst again and again.

Thirst can have so many meanings and nuances.

What if Jesus meant, "My strength comes from something beyond your understanding. Some force that is always there. Something that can help you to transcend your thirst?" What He said was, "The water I give is like an artesian spring within, gushing fountains of endless life."

She says something like, "I want some of that water!" But I think she thought something like, "I don't ever want to have to come back to this well again. That way I don't have to see people's scorn or deal with them gossiping behind my back."

We so often miss the true depth and breadth of what Jesus is saying to us.

Jesus is offering the woman a lot more than just a drink of water. The story goes on and He shows her that He knows all about her life and her choices. He does know the depths of her well, but He didn't condemn her. He just stated it as fact.

He understood who she was. And He *still* offered her gushing fountains of endless life—if she chose to take His offer.

Jesus wants us to live a life <u>worth</u> living. He died so we can *live*.

I've had good intentions, but like the woman at the well, I underestimated Jesus. I, too, would have thought my well was too deep for Him to draw anything meaningful from it.

Yet, in kindness and with patience, He showed the woman at the well—and me—understanding. He did not judge. He provided a better way. Jesus didn't ask the woman at the well to erase her past either. I thought I might have to erase my past or cover it up. I thought I needed to continue carrying my shame.

But in the story, Jesus showed her love that allowed her to embrace who she was as well as who she could become. That grace, love, and forgiveness helped her see herself in a more complete light. Jesus's love accepted her for where she'd been, what she'd been through, and for who she was because of it.

I believe Jesus sees our hearts. He knows our motives. He sees them clearly. And He operates, I believe, from a place of love.

I had a choice to make, just like the woman at the well did. Would I let my past go or would I let it define me? Would I choose to let the weight stay off my shoulders or would I pick it all back up again?

There's one more quick story that leads me to believe Jesus wants the weight to stay off. There is another woman, documented in Luke 7, that pours expensive perfume on Jesus's feet. She causes quite the stir. A religious leader, a Pharisee, who is at the dinner says to himself, "If this man is the prophet He claims to be, He would have known what kind of woman this is falling all over him."

People don't want to let us forget our mistakes.

I encourage you to read Luke 7. Jesus gets very specific in this story. He dresses the leaders down quite blatantly while holding her up because He saw her heart and her motives. Jesus sees what is truly going on in every situation. Jesus finishes by telling her, "Your sins are forgiven. Your faith has saved you; go in peace."

So, I believe Jesus would say, "Let it go. I died so that you may have peace."

See why these passages spoke to me?

31

n the time that's passed since meeting Jesus in my bathtub, I have begun to see the metaphor He meticulously painted with His life. Uncovering that metaphor has changed my life.

He came to show that God is *love*, not hate and violence and selfish agendas. Those things come out of our brokenness, what we need to be saved from. Jesus revealed this beautiful, loving picture of what life could be like if I chose to recognize that love.

I humbled myself that night in my bathtub and realized that I am not the end-all and be-all of the universe. I don't deserve squat. I don't deserve to act like a jerk in the grocery store line, for example, because the cashier isn't moving fast enough. Because I understand that my rights are not more important than others. I'm living for the greater good now.

I don't deserve special treatment.

No one deserves special treatment.

Jesus said He came to serve.

Isn't *deserve* the exact opposite?

Let's look at another metaphor. Take the story of Adam and Eve in the Garden of Eden. In Genesis, Adam and Eve were given everything they needed to sustain life. They had a purpose and a reason for living. Adam got to name all of creation. Eve got to tend to the garden. What more could they want? Their purposes ebbed and flowed and changed with the needs of their environment. That gave Adam and Eve variety and choices. Yet, when tempted by the serpent, Eve, then Adam, didn't hesitate. They immediately chose their own agenda.

Can you see the metaphor?

We are Adam and Eve. Their story is our story.

We struggle for independence from our Creator. We eat from the tree of knowledge of good and evil because we're not satisfied in the passenger seat. We want our eyes to be open, but we are unprepared for the consequences of that knowledge. Part of the metaphor, I believe, is that we brought evil into our own lives.

Why was the tree or the temptation even there? Because that's life. It's real. We all get to choose. I believe it was God's wish that we wouldn't choose evil. Jesus didn't choose evil. Jesus lived according to God's will. God wants us to *choose* life and love, but we want to be in control of our own lives, and we are unprepared for what that really means.

Why did God give us choices? Because to choose is so much better than being forced. God won't force us to do anything. Our choices are our classroom.

It seems to me that God stands close by and offers us a hand as He says, "Take it, let me lead. We will get through this together and I will give you life abundant."

However, people continue to paint a picture of a revenge-seeking god. Yet God continues to show love with a straining, outstretched hand, as portrayed in Michelangelo's painting, the Creation of Adam. Jesus, who is the new Adam, chose the way of love, justice, mercy, and compassion instead of self, and reverses what happened in Eden.

Can you see the metaphor?

Adam is translated to "man." So, Jesus is the "new man," if you will. I believe this is pointing to this idea of renewal through Christ; Regenerate man.

I think we can all agree Jesus of Nazareth was a real person who lived a real life. He was quoted saying in John 17:21, "As the Father and I are one, may you all be one with each other." He showed us that self has no place in the Kingdom of God. Even the concept of our Creator is not one-self, but a triune God of body, mind, and spirit.

> We are to love our neighbor as we love ourselves, because we are new beings.

I believe God was in that fraternity house with me over thirty years ago.

I believe God was with me eight years later, both in that operating room and in that cold, lonely hallway.

I believe God was with me six long years after that. And He led me to Jesus in my bathtub because I was finally ready to hear about the peace God brought— peace the world didn't seem to know anything about.

God had pursued me the whole time. He just waited for me to clear my eyes through surrender, so I could stop seeing people as trees.[7] In other words, God wanted me to stop seeing people as objects to be used at my discretion. He wanted me to cease mindless pleasure seeking and do something productive with my life.

God wanted me to value myself and learn discretion and self-control. He wanted me to start taking responsibility for my actions, and to stop expecting other people to make me happy or try to control and manipulate their actions in order to fit my expectations. God wants this for everyone. God wants us all to understand that we are loved so that we can move beyond mere survival and make a difference, help other people, and be like Jesus to someone else.

God asked me to stop focusing on me, me, *me*.

The Zac Brown Band and Jimmy Buffet say: "When you lose yourself, you find the key to paradise!"[8]

It seems as if the key to a fulfilled, fully lived, abundant life was presented the moment I gave up on me.

32

he only critique I have concerning the story of the woman at the well is, it stops before we get to the part about how she might begin to live her new-found, facade-free, transformed, abundant life. We see the first part, where she encounters Jesus and He gives light to a better way. But what happened after that? How did she live her life after meeting Jesus?

I go back to the renewal of the mind. It's one thing to be "saved." It's completely different to live your life in relationship with Jesus. People serve and love Jesus every day and still sin. I'm not saying it's okay, I'm saying it's reality.

That's what I love about the thought of renewal through relationship. It feels active to me. To be reborn is one thing, but that seems stagnant. To stay on the path of transformation, because of that relationship, is quite another.

Jesus said, "Go and sin no more." That's where I get real. Like I stated earlier, I continue to sin. Sin basically means we miss the mark. I miss the mark daily. Sometimes I miss the mark minute to minute, it just depends on the day! I believe there is just one sin and it is missing the mark of what is acceptable to God. So, anything that makes us miss our mark with God is sin.

I understand Jesus says, "Go and sin no more," So, since I still get mad, or gossip, or covet, or revert to selfishness, and don't do what God wants me to do, does that mean I cannot follow Jesus's teachings? Does that mean I'm not following Him? I have a story that leads me to my answer—at least one that's sufficient for me.

Peter, first called Simon, was a fisherman and one of the first disciples Jesus called to follow Him, which he did for three years. In the end, Peter denied three times even knowing Jesus. That was after swearing to Jesus's face he would never deny knowing Him. Then, after Jesus was crucified, Peter went back to his old life. He didn't understand anything Jesus tried to tell him. Peter missed the mark several times, but Jesus knew the guilt and shame Peter placed on his own shoulders, so Jesus gave Peter the chance to redeem himself three times. Is that a coincidence? I don't think so.

John 21:1–19 describes when Jesus appeared to seven of the disciples at the Sea of Galilee. He invited them over to the fire to warm themselves and share a meal. With love, Jesus told Peter what he needed to do to move forward and to live out his purpose. Peter was to feed Jesus's sheep, which meant he was to build the Church—the body of Christ.

Jesus knew Peter had gone back to his old life and that he was disoriented and unsure of what had even been asked of him. But Jesus met Peter where he was, on the beach, and roasted fresh fish for them. After coming back in from casting their nets, Jesus invites the disciples to, "Come and have breakfast."

It seems to me that Jesus wanted Peter back.

There was no confrontation. Nor did Jesus say, "Shame on you, Peter!"

Instead, Jesus gave Peter the chance to turn around, nourish himself, commune with Jesus, and then get back to work. You gotta love Jesus!

Should our spiritual goal be to decrease in sin or to increase in our relationship with Jesus? [9]

33

While many may accuse me of moving too slow, or even moving backward, I'm okay with that. Many stories of faith speak of someone who meets Jesus and their life is instantly transformed. That's not my story, but I'm happy with the process of my transformation and the fact that it's not happening easily or overnight. Many *aha!* moments haven't been that big at all. Instead, they have been seemingly insignificant snippets revealed to me; Like the manna the Israelites received in the desert.[10] Tomorrow always had to wait until tomorrow. With each day, more of the puzzle will continue to fill itself in.

But I want you to hear me on this: I truly believe I am shorting myself by still continuing to try to refill at empty wells. I still don't have my poop entirely in a group. And I've been putting this book off, I realized, thinking that one of these days I was going to be all together. But I'm no longer sure it will happen on this side of life. And I don't think waiting any longer is what I'm supposed to do. Because God is seen as great when He works through weak people. So even though I haven't stopped gossiping, drinking, smoking, swearing, getting angry, lusting after what I don't have, et cetera, et cetera, I'm publishing this book!

Even though I don't get to tie my story up in a pretty package with a beautiful bow, I'm writing my story, unapologetically! Maybe it will help those whose paths have been much straighter to understand that those of us who struggle believe Jesus sees us and loves us too!

I've discovered life isn't about calming storms, it's about how we ride through the storms and still manage to find and create love and light despite our circumstances.

So, how does this peace manifest itself in my life? What have I taken on or given up in order to keep this peace? What has changed in me? I'm giving you what has worked for me. But remember, I am practicing! I don't get any of them correct all the time, but I press on toward the goal!

I worship only God.

I do not worship myself, money, people, habits, or things. I have to think about this one a lot to keep myself on track. I try to stay centered on who is important. And I talk to God a lot.

I believe Jesus.

Not just or only *in* Jesus. I also believe the red letters and I allow them to speak truth and life to me and they show me the way to real, authentic, non-conformist, abundant *life*.

I get on my knees and pray.

I usually whine and fuss about whatever is going on in my life first, but then I get on my knees and give it to God. I do this in private, usually in the shower. This is also where I do some of my best thinking and reflecting, which will bring me to my knees.

When faced with a dire situation, I try to acknowledge that there is love and goodness out there. Love never fails. For me, prayer aligns me with that goodness, light, and love.

I let go of expectations.

I used to have expectations for the people in my life—pretty much all the people in my life. And most of those expectations had to do with me. I wanted my kids to make me look good. I wanted my spouse to act exactly how I thought he should. For the longest time, I was so frustrated, and I couldn't figure out why. One day, my counselor said, "You expect your husband to take care of you, but he cannot. Only you can take care of you!"

I realized I gave all my power to others and I expected something in return. For a control freak, that was a pretty silly thing to do! I let something I had no control over at all—what others will and won't do or think—determine my direction and mood.

Giving up expectations also meant I had to give up pride. People kind of confuse pride. Giving it up doesn't mean you have no confidence or goals; it's just the opposite. I have greater confidence in my decisions and goals because I gave up those expectations, which no person ever filled anyway. Listening to that still, small voice, I move forward. When I have a peace in my heart and there hasn't been roadblock after roadblock put in front of the decision, I move forward with confidence.

I finally learned that my expectations were part of my selfish agenda. When I stopped putting expectations on people—only on myself—my life became a much happier place to live! I'm taking care of myself and letting others do the same. When I have days where not a lot of joy is to be found, I check my expectations and can usually find the answer there.

I've learned to pick my battles.

Some battles are worth fighting. Others are not. Many times when someone has offended us, it's really about expectations, or believing we deserve something better. I have found that when I am able to stand back, not respond immediately, and work my emotions out before I choose whether to fight or not, most battles simply disappear. My mood changes quickly, I don't give into fear and I remember that I can only control *my* behavior and attitude.

I let my "give a damn" break and I don't intend on fixing it.

This one completely depends on how well you love yourself! When I can hold my tongue, as an example, and not respond to someone's hurtful jab or whatever gets thrown my way, I am usually able to let it go and not obsess over the situation all day. By not allowing myself to get sucked in and then replay it in my head over and over again, I am able to forget it faster. Nothing escaped my scrutiny before. Every battle had to be fought. My brain was a lot like the news and it had 24/7 coverage. No wonder I couldn't move on, forgive, and let go of that.

When I choose to let something go for the sake of the relationship, I am able to move on quickly. When I choose to talk only to God about it, I am able to remain peace- and joy-filled because He tempers my attitude, and I see things from a different perspective. Then, I am able to enjoy the time I have with the person I am with or enjoy whatever task I'm working on. I wrecked too many days because my pride would not let anything slide. A dear friend used to say, "Take it to the throne, not the phone!"[11]

That seems like a small thing, doesn't it? The magnitude of this concept, however, is nearly overwhelming to me. Imagine being in a place where you can give up control, let go of pride and useless expectations, and just let things slide. That's the key, isn't it? That's the magnitude of which I speak. Be okay while letting things slide. Even though I still struggle with control, I know that calm is possible in the midst of the storm. Most times I think I achieve that calm. I no longer take things personally.

I surrender the situation.

Part of what I talked about under "picking your battles" is applicable here. When I surrender a situation, I give it to God. I see myself handing it over. Sometimes, I take it right back, but I try to give it up. Again and again, if need be! I pray about the situation after that. I'll give you an example:

My daughter has not always made great choices in friends. During different times in her life, I have worried about that. I've talked with her about it. I've tried to boost her self-esteem. I have talked with her about her worth in God's eyes. Then finally, probably more out of desperation than anything, I prayed about it.

"God, I give up. I can't do anything in this situation. Help! Bring new people into her life." Once I truly let go, more got done. My nerves are much calmer, and I can focus on doing things I can accomplish. My attitude changed. My daughter's friends have changed, too.

I remember Jesus was a real man.

When I am at my lowest, and people are at their meanest, I remember Jesus experienced life on earth just as we are right now. He knew joy and passion, fun and laughter, sorrow, heartache, and disappointment. He experienced love and hypocrisy. He spent time with the learned and the ignorant, just like you and me. He experienced even more than we will likely see in our lifetime and yet he knew how to calm the sea. He was undeterred by people around him.

I assume the best in people.

Instead of thinking the worst of people, I choose to stay positive and assume they want what's best, even if their best doesn't agree with what I think is best. This freed up unbelievable amounts of space in my head. I wasn't thinking about how people were out to get me, or wanted to hurt me, or prove me wrong. I don't need to worry about revenge.[12]

I figured out what worked for me and what didn't.

I thought long and hard after everything I had allowed into my life surfaced as my tipping point. I thought about what was okay and what wasn't. I spent a long time building a wall, but I was missing boundaries from my life. I believe boundaries are missing for a lot of people whose parents were narcissists, alcoholics or substance abusers.

After I realized the power of healthy boundaries, I enforced them. (It took a while. There was a definite learning curve!) Healthy boundaries give you confidence about your life and your choices. Perhaps even more important, they give you space to be truly compassionate. When I was all worked up because I got myself into a mess due to lack of boundaries, I couldn't have cared less what was going on with me, you, or anyone else.

When someone crosses one of my boundaries and I don't stick up for myself, I am frustrated, angry, passive aggressive, not fully engaged, and not assuming the best of them. When I uphold the things that I need to keep me in my peaceful state, I am centered, able to be fully present, engaged, happy, calm, and kind. I am joy-filled. I am at one with God.

I gave up the notion that everyone must think and act like me.

Giving up this notion meant I had to give up pride and the belief that my thoughts are everyone else's thoughts, too. Isn't this why we argue? We believe we are right, and we want to show the other person how flawed their thinking is and get them to think the way we do. That is pride.

The world needs all kinds of people, perceptions, races, creeds, nationalities, genders, and orientations. Everyone is welcome in God's kingdom. We need to make room for them. Everyone wants the same things I want: love and acceptance.

This has had practical implications on my life. For one thing, I no longer feel the need to prove I am right. I am able to let people think what they are going to think and to let things go much easier.

My relationship with the offender is what I find ultimately important now—more important than proving I am right. It's more important than trying to persuade someone to my way of thinking or trying to fix them or their "faulty" ideology.[13]

Jesus was always about relationship.

I let people have their own opinion of me.

I used to try to carefully script what anyone might think or say about me. Now I respect the fact that they can think anything they want. I am not going to change their opinion. It's really none of my business what they think. It doesn't make me who I am. It doesn't make their opinions about me true.

I take time to serve.

Whether it's listening when a friend needs me, opening the door for someone, or going on a mission trip, I try to serve someone else for no reason other than to do it. With no pay, and no benefit to me, I try to just do something good for someone else. What I find in serving, is that there is a *huge* benefit to me—my soul is filled with good things. It's a wonderful way to recharge.

I take self-care seriously.

I practice yoga. I work out. I try to eat healthy, whole foods and I try to eat the bad stuff only once in a while. But, I eat what I want to eat. I take a supplement daily to make sure my body gets what it needs. I also get away when I need to, even if it's just forty-five minutes to Lake Michigan for the day. Perhaps most important for me is I have made my home a haven—a place of respite for me and others.

Do the stuff that fills your soul with joy. Whether it's going to dinner with friends, reading a great book, taking a walk, or going on a road trip, there are ways to take in the beauty that is all around us. Whatever it may be, if it's light bearing, do it.

I also think it's important to get yourself a group of people you can honestly do life with. It doesn't necessarily have to be a church, but it may be of most help if it's of a spiritual nature. You want to be part of a community that loves, serves, and shares together. The best part of my second marriage was the season we chose to be part of a small group. We did life together. Those were good, fulfilling times. I honestly can't remember why we no longer thought it was important. Most likely we felt like we got too busy. That's ironic now.

I don't allow people to infect me with their negativity.

I know whose I am and what that means for my life. If you want to pee in my Wheaties, just know, I won't give you the payoff you're looking for. I take a deep breath and figure that person is hurting more than I am.

Anyway, look to the bright side of life, my friends. Remember, self-pity and negative spirits are not productive. And what you think on, you become.

I've learned about fear.

I look back and can see that fear motivated my actions and reactions most times. When I did something defensive or shot a defensive jab, it was because I was worried about self-preservation and making sure I didn't get hurt.

When you set yourself aside, you don't worry about self-preservation, so your fear can subside. Now, I have a peace about most things in my life and I am able to see the difference between worldly pride and real confidence. I can see fear everywhere I look, and I believe it motivates a lot of us.

I've learned about self-control.

Faithfulness is slowly replacing my impetuous nature. Patience is replacing my frustration. Joy is replacing my anger. Prosperity is replacing my hardship. Generosity toward others has become possible because I no longer squander what has been given to me. Part of that self-control is learning to capture those thoughts that come into our heads; Thoughts of greed and idolatry, lust and temptation, anger and defense, and fear and contempt. I believe I recognize those thoughts much more quickly in myself and I repent of them. I want to put them down and move forward without them.

I am much slower to anger.

I can still let my humanness get the best of me, but for the most part, I take a deep breath, I shut my mouth, and I walk away, or keep scrolling, if I have to. I no longer allow myself to get mad enough to consider revenge or murder. I wish I would have learned this skill earlier in my life. Many interactions would have gone much smoother.

I try very hard to not covet.

It can be easy to look at friends and neighbors and be jealous of what we believe they have—possessions or relationships they have been able to attain. I try to be happy for them and remember they worked hard, instead of allowing myself to feel jealous. I also under-stand that things are rarely ever completely as they seem.

I am authentic.

I remind myself that God does not love me for what I do, but for who I am—who I was made to be—and who I am still becoming. I still need to work on this one. It can be hard to be vulnerable, especially after being hurt because of your vulnerability. But let your freak flag fly! Let it fly indeed. There's no one else like you. Your story can only become useful for someone else when you are truly authentic.

I try not to gossip.

I do still talk about people sometimes, but I try to make it positive and I don't repeat or spread rumors. I put a lot of effort into this one. When I spent a lot of time getting frustrated or angry with people about what they were or weren't doing, it affected my peace.

I don't judge.

In reality, we all judge others in some way or another—we just do. However, when I gave up feeling as if I had to rescue or fix someone, I was able to settle down and hear what they were saying. I can easily choose to walk alongside people because I have put away my judgments.[13] I would rather love and walk beside others than judge and point at them from afar.

All judgments lead to division and hatred. If everyone just realized that we are all hypocrites, and in need of something to save us from our overindulged selves, people might respond to truth, the real way, and life, a bit differently. I think most of us would agree that life should primarily be about our own transformation, and letting God worry about and help with the rest of the world's transformation. I'm not saying don't do what needs to be done, I just wrote about serving others, I'm saying mind your own business.

I wonder if anything offends Jesus as much as us? I believe what we see as differences matter very little to Him. I believe He sees the heart alone. He sees "it" in all of us and says He is the one who can judge, yet He still chooses love, not wrath. Jesus sees even more. He wants us to see even more. All the stuff we get worked up over—the stuff we see in each other that we want to judge and point out as wrong—is missing the mark. The people Jesus got most angry with were the hypocrites whose hearts were closed off, to learning and to repentance.

He wants to love us into a good relationship with our Creator, universe, others, and self.

How about instead of treating people with contempt because of their thorn, we meet them with compassion? What kind of world would that look like? I know I desire compassion from others, so why is that compassion so difficult to give?

Our priorities should be: humility, patience, love, justice, mercy, and compassion. How do we show love when we hate, judge, and condemn? How do we show justice when we prohibit others from basic human rights? How do we show mercy when we ignore millions of people who are slaughtered all over the world? How do we show compassion when we let our neighbors go hungry or worse yet, try to prohibit people from even becoming our neighbor?

I knew I needed to stop playing God. I am not an appropriate judge. There will always be a sector of people who think a certain way. There will always be a sector of people who think that way is horrible and needs to be stopped. But we must stop trying to legislate morality. If God gave us choices and free will, then we all should get to exercise our rights to choose and to have free will. We live in a world that perpetually misses the mark. No amount of law or legislation will save us from ourselves.

We need to stop hating and judging and believing ourselves superior. We need to love all people exactly the way they are. One can hope that through those actions of love, people can get a glimpse of a loving God. That's how you show someone hope. You won't judge them into your way of thinking. It doesn't work that way.

I realized that I am here for a greater purpose than just being happy.

To start this section, I need you to understand that it doesn't come easily to me to give up my selfish ways. I have to choose this daily, and there have been days and periods in my life when I have chosen my happiness over anything else.

You might be thinking, "I get choosing happiness, because giving up your right to yourself sounds scary and crazy." Think about what I said in my bit about picking your battles, not judging, and my purpose not necessarily being linked to my happiness. Think about all those bold statements that you've read. None of them would have been possible unless and until I gave up my right to myself. I tried it by myself. I ran my life into multiple ditches when I thought I could do it on my own.

Until you live in a surrendered position, I believe you will fight, but you will not find true peace in the midst of the storm. When I chose happiness over integrity and God's will in my life, I thought I deserved something. I was judgmental, and I was no longer authentic. I was covetous. I worshipped myself. I didn't assume the best of people. I was no longer living surrendered. My life came to a crashing halt, but, as Monty Python says, "I got better!

I've cut loose the baggage that goes with keeping up the facade.

All that is important in a superficial sense. I've stated it before, but it bears repeating here, Oswald Chambers says in the Opposition of the Natural, "This is where the battle has to be fought. The things that are right, noble, and good [in the world's eyes] are the very things that keep us from being God's best."

The ability to let go of shame and criticism, and the superficiality that comes from trying to hide them, in order to spend time on more productive ventures is what leads to peace in the middle of the storm too.

Since I started following Jesus, I've broken free from the facade and developed authentic relationships, and sought authentic justice, mercy, and compassion. For me, only when I am rightly related with Him am I rightly related with others and operating out of love and not fear. Fear leads to the facade.

Nothing I've said in this book can set you free. You may become more enlightened or perhaps look at something from a new perspective, but I cannot set you free. You can't set yourself free either. If you could, you would have by now.

Are you going to continue fumbling around in the dark?

Only after my eyes were cleared and I began to embrace my vulnerabilities was I able to see the bigger agenda. I realize only when my self-will is surrendered, and I'm relating to others out of love, am I "not far from the Kingdom of God."

I've become humbler and less self-righteous.

When we lose our humility and become self-righteous, we drive ourselves into ditches. My life with Jesus just isn't neat and tidy. I used to think it was. The truth is, I was so wrapped up in my own righteousness—and this isn't easy for me to admit—I couldn't see when I went wrong. I became a pride-filled person again when I lost touch with humility. I didn't recognize myself again. My friends didn't recognize me, nor did my ex-husband.

I know now that my relationship with Jesus is messy. It's a bit of a conundrum. But I no longer take it for granted. I still falter, yet I believe that He is the way, the truth, and the life. My faith is something I both possess and work toward. My journey isn't finished though. My journey isn't even close to complete, it's ever unfolding.

I continue to miss the mark, yet I continue. I keep moving forward. I fall down and scrape my knee. At times, I've broken my leg. Yet I rise and brush off the gravel and dirt. I hold my head up, even if it hurts, or I am ashamed. And I walk on. I put one foot in front of the other, not because I can, but because Jesus wants me to. And He gives me the strength to do so.

The only way the enemy wins is if he keeps you down. If he keeps you looking down, doubting yourself, questioning yourself, and letting others' opinions define who you are.

Jesus wants us to take the moments we need to rest. He wants us to nourish ourselves, and then to get up, keep going,[14] and to live our best lives now, cuz this ain't no dress rehearsal!

Grace and peace to you, my friend!

ENDNOTES

1   John 4:1-26

2   "Animal Spirit Guides: The Owl, "http://www.psychicguild.com/articles_view.php?id=707, January 2011.

3   Barbara Fay, Retired United Methodist pastor.

4   Charles Stanley, First Baptist Church, Atlanta GA (now retired)

5   Inspired by David Crowder Band's "Wholly Yours."

6   Oswald Chambers, "The Opposition of the Natural," *My Utmost for His Highest,* http:/utmost.org/the-opposition-of-the-natural.

7   Mark 8:22-26 (NIV).

8   Zac Brown Band's "Knee Deep."

9   Kyle Randall, pastor and friend.

10   Exodus 16 (NIV).

11   Kristi Ransbottom, friend and mentor.

12   Inspired by Brene Brown

13   Inspired by John Pavlovitz, *The Bigger Table.*

14   1 Kings 19:5.